Interdisciplinary Teaching Through Games and Activities

John G. Helion, Ed.D.
Frank F. Fry, Jr. , D.P.E.
West Chester University

Dad,
A lot of water has passed
under the bridge since we
were together. You have continued
to improve and I hope you
never stop!
Frank

KENDALL/HUNT PUBLISHING COMPANY
4050 Westmark Drive   Dubuque, Iowa 52002

Copyright © 2003 by John G. Helion and Frank F. Fry

ISBN 0-7575-0275-X

Printed in the United States of America
10 9 8 7 6 5 4 3 2 1

I would like to take this opportunity to thank my wife, Ann and my daughters, Courtney and Chelsea, for their continued love, understanding and support during this project. I would also like to thank all the students, past and present, at West Chester University who contributed their time and effort to the creation, modification and testing of many of the activities in this book.

John G. Helion, Ed.D

This book is dedicated to my wife, Marcia, for her unfailing support throughout my career; to my boys, Tyler and Kyle, for being so understanding when told, "Daddy's got to work" and to my parents for their love, support and guidance. My thanks also goes to those students who invested their time and effort in my classes at West Chester University. Thank you all!

Frank F. Fry, D.P.E.

Table of Contents

Introduction

The intricate interplay among the three components in education: the student, the teacher and the curricular content, requires a dynamic balancing act on the part of all concerned. The teacher holds the dominant role and can be the facilitator of a rich educational experience for all whom they contact. This is the desire of all dedicated professionals in the field of education regardless of the grade or age group.

The ultimate goal of any educational undertaking is the advancement of learning. While giving us some clues, research concerning teaching has been unsuccessful in pinpointing the actual components that guarantee student learning in all instances. Something that has been established is the fact that learners process information using three modalities: auditory, visual and kinesthetic/tactile. While we utilize all three of these modalities as learners, one usually predominates. It is through this primary learning modality that we as learners best process information. In the past, much of the education in the classroom utilized the auditory and visual modalities. While the lecture and demonstration format of this type of learning worked well for many, the kinesthetic/tactile learners, at times, struggled. Trends toward the use of manipulatives in the classroom to address this problem have greatly enhanced achievement for these students.

Addressing the beneficial dissemination of information in the form of the existing district curriculum is our mandate. The individual approach, teaching style, and method of delivery are normally at the discretion of the teacher. Finding what works best for the students should be foremost in our minds. Unfortunately, and all too often, what works for the educator, and in some cases what is easiest, dominates the learning atmosphere. Good teaching requires effort from all parties involved. Cooperation between teacher and student makes learning more successful and fun for everybody!

An inherent characteristic of children is their enjoyment of movement and play. Simply attend any Physical Education class and watch and listen to the responses of the children. Stand on the playground of any school during a free play period watch and listen. The psychomotor domain has for too long been overlooked by educators for its obvious benefits to the whole child. Parents can often be overheard telling their children that they wish they put as much time into their schoolwork as they do their play periods. Coaches can mesmerize groups of children for prolonged periods because children's physical engagement is considered enjoyable even though they are alleged to be learning how to play or improve in a particular sport activity.

The intent of this book is to take the natural enjoyment of children's play and games and put it into the context of their learning. The activities included in this text are intended to act as reinforcement vehicles for curricular content covered in the classroom. Once introduced in the classroom the information can then be incorporated in the context of their favorite environment: the playground, gymnasium and in a few cases the classroom. This book is in no way meant to be all inclusive of the potential for cognitive and psychomotor interplay. Rather it is intended to be the starting point from which an energetic and innovative educator can embellish a sound elementary curriculum. This becomes yet another vehicle for effective delivery of curricular content on the part of every dedicated professional educator. Good luck and remember there are no "Game Police;" modify anything you find in this book to make it most effective in your particular educational situation.

Chapter One

Why Use Activities?

Chapter Overview

This chapter explores the primary learning modalities and discusses their importance in the individual learner's acquisition of knowledge. Specific characteristics of each learning modality are presented and an activity that enables learners to identify their preferred learning modality is included.

Questions to Consider

1. What are the Learning Modalities?

2. How is student learning affected by the Learning Modalities?

3. How do the Learning Modalities affect teacher decision-making?

4. How can knowledge regarding Learning Modalities be used to enhance teaching and student learning?

5. What is my preferred learning modality and how does effect my performance as a teacher?

People process information in different ways. The manner used to present material will many times determine whether or not a person will successfully grasp the information being presented. There are a number of aspects to consider when conducting learning activities. Effective planning, allocated practice time at the proper level of difficulty, and specific feedback have been shown to improve student learning. The instructor must also, however, consider the primary learning modalities of the students.

The Primary Learning Modalities

There are three primary learning modalities. They are Visual, Auditory and Kinesthetic/Tactile. While each person uses all of the modalities for accessing and processing information, one of these modalities usually predominates.

The Visual Modality

A person who processes information visually needs to see actual examples of what is being presented. This can be in the form of diagrams, detail drawings, maps, exploded views or actual physical demonstration. They like vivid descriptions and will often try to visualize what they are hearing in their mind. They are highly attuned to the shape and appearance of things including words and people. They will remember faces while forgetting names.

Their writing tends to be quite neat with well-formed letters and good word spacing. They are usually concerned with the appearance of their writing and drawing. Their drawing tends to be quite detailed. While generally undisturbed by sounds in their environment, they are distracted by a lack of visual order or extraneous movement in the general area.

These learners tend to be organized and deliberate in their planning. They organize through writing and creating lists. Because of their tendency toward the visual, during periods of inactivity they will have a tendency to doodle or daydream. In new situations, they have a need to closely examine the structure of the environment.

Because they are less sensitive to auditory or kinesthetic modalities they tend to express their feelings through their physical expressions. Facial expressions are an especially accurate indicator of their mood. Art is preferred over music, due to its visual stimulus. Visual learners tend to be quiet, getting restless during long verbal discourses. They are usually quite neat tending to have a strong sense of order. They may often refer to the visual when talking.

The Auditory Modality

A person who is an auditory processor relies on hearing the information that is to be acquired. This type of learner tends to be quite successful in a class that uses a lecture format. They will seek out detailed explanations and are easily distracted by noises. They may actually be observed talking themselves through situations. They sound out words when spelling, using a phonetic approach and may talk themselves through writing during the learning process. Unlike the visual learner, the auditory learner tends to remember names rather than faces. Auditory repetition serves to help with memorization.

As might be expected, auditory learners are easily distracted by sounds. They have "rabbit ears" so to speak. They will be constantly looking up to see what going on or who's passing by. They will usually solve problems by talking them out with the other person or talking themselves through problems.

Emotions are expressed with yells, cheers, screams, and squeals of delight. Moods can be determined by listening to the intonation of their words and phrases. Rather than looking mad, happy or sad, they will sound that way. While not as meticulous as visual processors, they can explain why they choose certain clothes; their appearance is not of great importance.

Again, because of the reliance on the auditory senses, music tends to be the preferred form of art for this type of learner.

The Kinesthetic/Tactile Modality

These learners are doers. They learn most efficiently by actually performing the skill they are trying to learn or by physically disassembling and re-assembling something they are trying to understand. They are experiential learners. It helps them to experience the feel of what they are trying to learn.

They enjoy action books. Their writing starts out fine generally but it has a tendency to deteriorate as they become short of space. They tend to use a great deal of pressure on their pens or pencils. They remember what they actually do. Things that they hear or see are not as well remembered. Since they are not as receptive to visual or auditory stimuli, they may seem to be distracted many times.

These people like to get their hands on things when faced with a challenge. They will try to do something physically to solve problems and at times act quite impulsively. They will fidget and find reasons to move about. They have a difficult time sitting still. In new situations they will reach out to touch, pick up, or try out something.

They are quite demonstrative emotionally. They are huggers and jumpers, stompers and pounders. Their body tone will usually be a good indicator of their mood. They talk with their hands. Gesturing is an important part of their communication process. Their need to get physically involved often creates the appearance of being rumpled although they start the day looking quite neat.

Implication for Teachers

One might wonder why the topic of primary learning modalities should be covered in this book. It is covered because it has a direct impact on both teaching and learning. Teachers and the pupils they work with all have their own preferred modalities.

Not only do we process information more efficiently through one of the modalities, but also as teachers we will have a tendency to present lessons primarily using our preferred modality. Auditory teachers are most comfortable using a lecture format. Visual teachers use more diagrams, overhead projectors and illustrations. Kinesthetic teachers tend to gesture and demonstrate more. Teaching using primarily one modality, can have a negative impact on the learning of students who do not share the same preferred modality as the teacher. Because of this, teachers must be aware of the different needs and modalities of their students and must plan lessons that address all three modalities, not merely the one with which they themselves are most comfortable. This does not mean that the teacher must know each individual students preferred modality. This only means that the teacher needs to be aware that different students require different approaches and incorporate activities into the lessons designed to address these various modalities.

Contextually Based Learning

There has been a great deal of study into the way the brain processes information and how learning takes place. Facilitating the learning process has been an ongoing challenge in all educational endeavors. It has been found that the brain can many times be compared to a large data bank. All the experiences of our lives are stored at either the conscious or subconscious levels. This is an important point to remember when considering ways to enhance student learning.

When presented with new information, the brain in an effort to better understand it, searches through the memory in an attempt to identify the new material based on what it has already experienced. The new information is compared to previously learned material in an attempt to categorize it for easier use. It is not uncommon to hear a person say, "Give me an example." or "Is it like...?", when someone is trying to explain a new situation to him or her.

This will effect how teachers structure learning experiences. If we can successfully call on our students past knowledge, we can help them acquire new material. This requires improved planning on the part of the teacher. The teacher must analyze the material to be covered and look for ways in which it resembles previously learned material. For the purposes of this book, one way to accomplish this could be to put the new material in the context of a physical activity.

This strategy can place the concepts being presented in a context that the students can more easily understand. Since children are usually familiar with the various aspects of game play and the relationship of the participant and their interaction, the physical experience of going through the actions can many times clarify or help students acquire new or difficult concepts.

Instead of the new material being presented in isolation with no relationship to any previous knowledge being identified, new ideas or material are juxtaposed against previously learned material in an effort to give them more substance and definition. This type of action increases the likelihood of student learning and understanding, since the new ideas are integrated neatly into the data bank of previous knowledge. Students know where these ideas "fit". If this is not done, if new ideas are presented in isolation, the student will still attempt to place the new knowledge based on their previous knowledge. This not only causes undue stress for students, but can also hinder the understanding process, since students may make an erroneous comparison, causing confusion and misunderstanding.

Exercise One

Modality Strength Checklist

In each of the fourteen following sections, check one of the descriptions that best represents your view of yourself. Each section has only one check possible. After cheching off one section, total the number of checks for Columns V, A and K. The column with the greatest number of checks broadly represents your preferred learning modality.

I/He/She	V VISUAL	A AUDITORY	K KINESTHETIC
LEARNING STYLE	Learns by seeing, watching and demonstrations.	Learns from verbal instruction from others or self.	Learns by doing, direct involvement.
READING	Likes descriptions, sometimes stops reading to stare into space and imagine scene; intense concentration.	Enjoys dialogue, plays; avoids lengthy descriptions; unaware of illustrations; moves lips or subvocalizes.	Prefers stories where action occurs early; fidgets when reading, handles books, not an avid reader.
SPELLING	Recognizes words by sight.; relies on configuration of words.	Uses phonics approach; has auditory word attack skills.	Often a poor speller, writes words to determine if they "feel" right.
HAND WRITING	Tends to be good, particularly when young; spacing and size are good; appearance is important.	Has more difficulty learning in initial stages; tends to write lightly; says strokes when writing.	Good initially, deteriorates as space becomes smaller; pushes harder on writing implement.
MEMORY	Remembers faces, forgets names; writes things down, takes notes.	Remembers names, forgets faces; remembers by auditory repetition.	Remembers best what was done, not what was seen or talked about.
IMAGERY	Vivid imagination; thinks in pictures, visualizes in detail.	Sub-vocalizes; thinks in sounds; details less important.	Imagery not important. Images that do occur are accompanied by movement.
DISTRACTABILITY	Generally unaware of sounds; distracted by visual disorder or movement.	Easily distracted by sounds.	Not attentive to visual, auditory presentation so seems distractable.
PROBLEM SOLVING	Deliberate; plans in advance; organizes thoughts by writing them; lists problems.	Talks problems out; tries solutions verbally, sub-vocally; talks self through problems.	Attacks problems physically; impulsive; often selects solutions involving greatest activity.
RESPONSE TO PERIODS OF INACTIVITY	Stares, Doodles, finds something to watch.	Hums, talks to self or others.	Fidgets, finds reasons to moves, holds up hands.

7

	V	A	K
RESPONSE TO NEW SITUATIONS	Looks around, examines structure.	Talks about situation, pros and cons, what to do.	Tries things out; touches, feels, manipulates.
EMOTIONALITY	Somewhat repressed; stares when angry; cries easily, beams when happy; facial expression is a good index of emotion.	Shouts with joy or anger; blows up verbally, but soon calms down; expresses emotions verbally and through changes in tone, volume and pitch of voice.	Jumps for joy; hugs, tugs and pulls when happy; stamps, jumps and pounds when angry; stomps off; body tone is a good index of emotion.
COMMUNICATION	Quiet; does not talk at length; becomes impatient when extensive listening is required; may use words clumsily; embellishes; uses words such as see, look, etc.	Enjoys listening, but cannot wait to talk; descriptions are long, but repetitive; likes hearing self and others talk; use words such as listen, hear etc.	Gestures when speaking; does not listen well; stands close when speaking or listening; quickly loses interest in detailed verbal discourse; uses words such as get, take, etc.
GENERAL	Neat; meticulous; likes order; may choose not to vary appearance.	Matching clothing not so important; can explain choices of clothing.	Neat, but soon becomes wrinkled through activity.
RESPONSE TO ARTS	Not particularly responsive to music; prefers the visual arts; tends not to voice appreciation on art of any kind, but can be deeply affected by visual displays; focuses on details and components rather than the work as a whole.	Favors music; finds less appeal in visual art, but is readily able to discuss it; misses significant detail but appreciates the work as a whole; is able to develop verbal association for all art forms; spends more time taking about pieces than looking at them.	Reponds to music by physical movement; prefers sculpture; touches statues and paintings; at exhibits stops only when she/he can become physically involved; comments little on any art form.
TOTAL NUMBER OF CHECKS IN EACH COLUMN (TOTAL MUST EQUAL 14)	V _____	A _____	K _____

Preferred Learning Modality is _____

Teaching Through Modality Strengths: Concepts and Practices. by Walter B. Barbe and Raymond H. Swassing, Zaner-Blosser, Inc.; Columbus, OH; 1979.

Chapter Two

Nuts and Bolts: Things You Need to Know and Things You Need to Make

1. Formations: How to group students into a variety of different formations in a quick and efficient manner.

2. Materials: How to make some of the special materials used for several of the activities in Chapter Four.

Grouping Students

The ability to organize students quickly and efficiently is important. This saves time that can be utilized in more student practice that can eventually lead to more student learning. One of the keys to this process is teaching the students various routines for dividing into the desired grouping in a simple manner. For the various activities in the book students will have to be grouped in various ways. Here are some suggestions for forming these groups.

Pairs/Partners/Two Teams

The most efficient way to achieve pair formation is to have the students find a partner! Anyone who has done this has realized that at times this may result in partnerships that may have trouble working well together. In this case, simply have everyone switch again and find another partner. To form two teams have partners number themselves "1" or "2". Ones become one team; two's become the other.

Get in Groups of...

To make groups of larger numbers or a certain number of groups it is usually fastest to instruct the class to get into groups of that number and number themselves within their group. For example, if you want four groups, have the students get into groups of four people and number themselves one through four. All the ones become a group; all the twos become another group and so on. This will result in four evenly numbered groups and can work for any number of groups. Extra students should come to the middle where they will number them selves and go to the appropriate team.

Using Playing Cards

One of the easiest and fun ways to group students is by using a standard deck of playing cards. Since most classes are smaller then 52 this becomes a quick and efficient ways to organize students into many different sized groups and have all children have the opportunity to work with each other.

Starting with aces give each student a playing card. Students then can then be grouped according to the value of their cards.

Two Teams – Two suites on one team, the other two suites on the second team; e.g. clubs and diamonds (team one), hearts and spades (team two) or odd and even numbers.
Three Teams – Three suites, divide the fourth among these three.
Four teams – Each suite becomes a group or use number values.
Partners – Same number, same color or same number, different color
Groups of Four – Students with the same number.

Counting Off

While this is the least efficient and most time consuming way of grouping students it is still one of the most widely used. Have the students line up and count down the row into groups of the desired number; e.g. If you want five groups, you would the students number themselves one through five until all children have a number.   After all have counted and received a number, the students get together with others of the same number. Be aware that many students get so involved in the act of counting that they forget their numbers! It is important that students remember their number or confusion and more wasted time will result.

Formations

Each game in this book will utilize some kind of starting formation. These formations are described and illustrated below.

Scatter - Students are randomly scattered throughout the playing area.

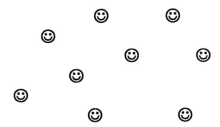

Line – Students are all in the same line. This may either be a file (one behind the other) or a rank (shoulder to shoulder).

Shuttle – Students are organized into several files. There should be no more than four in any file.

Scattered Pairs- Students are paired with another student. These pairs then randomly space themselves throughout the playing area.

Lined Pair – Students are paired with another student. Partners are designated "1" and "2". All "1"s line up shoulder to shoulder in a straight line. All "2"s form a similar line by standing across from and facing their partners.

☺☺☺☺☺☺☺☺☺☺☺☺
☺☺☺☺☺☺☺☺☺☺☺☺

Small Group - This is similar to a random formation except students are organized into a certain number of groups. The number of groups will be determined by the activity.

Materials

Some activities in this book require equipment not found in catalogues or typical school equipment rooms. These materials, however, are low cost and easily made. Some can even be used as class projects.

Clothespins

Whiles clothespins are readily available, they have to be modified for use in the various games in this book.

Materials – 200 or more wooden spring type clothespins. (The more the better)
              Thin point indelible markers of various colors

Preparation – Using the markers write one letter on each clothespin using the following frequency:

A – 9	B – 2	C – 2	D – 4	E – 12	F – 2
G – 3	H – 2	I – 9	J – 1	K – 1	L – 4
M – 2	N – 6	O – 8	P – 2	Q – 1	R – 6
S – 4	T – 6	U – 4	V – 2	W – 2	X – 1
Y – 2	Z – 1	Blank – 2			

On the other side of the clothespin write the name of a state, state capitol or major city. Countries, continents, rivers or any other pertinent material can also be written on the clothespins. This may be used as a classroom project enlisting the help of the students to assist in the preparation of the clothespins.

Carpet Squares

Carpet squares are invaluable. They can be used for skating activities and a wood or linoleum floor and just a soft place to sit when chairs are not available. It is sometimes possible to obtain carpet sample booklets from carpet distributors and showrooms. They may be given away free or sold at a nominal cost. You can phone the various carpet stores in your area and check availability and price. Carpet remnants are usually easy to find a good price. You can sometimes obtain used remnants from carpet dealers. These can be cut into various sizes. These should be cut into 1' x 2' sections allowing one for every child in the class with a few extra.

Carpet Skates

To make carpet skates cut* the carpet into 6" x 12" sections. You will need two for each student. Students can stand on these with the pile side down and shuffle across wood and linoleum floors.

*Note - Cutting carpet requires a sharp carpet knife and a straightedge. Carpet should be placed on a hard surface and care must be taken to avoid injury. The proper type of knife is available at all home centers or carpet outlets.

Chapter Three

Creating a Safe Learning Environment

Chapter Overview

This chapter explores the learning environment and it's impact on student acquisition of knowledge. The importance of physically and emotionally safe classroom settings and their effect on student risk taking behaviors and approach tendencies toward attempting new material will be looked at. The effects of stress on children and different ways this stress can be managed are discussed. Teacher responsibility and strategies for creating safe learning environments are also addressed.

Questions to Consider

1. Why is it important to run an emotionally and physically safe classroom?

2. How do you go about an emotionally/physically safe environment in you classroom?

3. What rules can you use to insure emotional/physical safety?

4. What is negligence and what can you do to guard against it?

If any classroom is to be productive, all the people in that particular environment must feel secure in the fact that they are safe to try new things and explore their own limits. In order to accomplish this, the classroom needs to be a place where both the student and the teacher feel safe to take risks. By risks, we do not means situations in which bodily safety is compromised or children are expected to attempt things that are inappropriate. Risk taking for our purposes means trying out new or different approaches designed to test and explore the limits of one's intellectual or physical potential.

If we expect our students to take risks and try new things in our classrooms[1], the classrooms must be places that foster exploration and inquiry. This can only be accomplished if our students feel both emotionally and physically safe. The teacher can and should take the necessary steps to foster this type of climate in the classroom.

Creating Emotional Safety

Teachers who create emotionally safe classrooms are concerned with the feelings of their students. Actions that belittle or embarrass another person in the class are not to be taken or tolerated. Put downs, comparisons and inappropriate competition are not a part of this type of learning environment. In an emotionally safe classroom, effort is celebrated regardless of the outcome and mistakes or failures are seen merely as feedback for future successes.

Rules for the Safe Classroom

Teachers concerned with the emotional safety of the learning environment need to be proactive in their attempts to create such a setting. There are a number of

---

[1]The word classroom refers to any environment or setting in which learning takes place; i.e. a classroom, gymnasium, field, playground, etc.

considerations that can be made toward this end. We suggest that you consider the following guidelines as a place to begin.

People Are Not for Hurting

This guideline is the one from which all others evolve. This is a rule that simply means that no action intended to hurt, shame, embarrass or belittle another person in the class is ever purposely taken by either the teacher or another student. This guideline includes both physical and verbal actions. While simple in definition, however, the practice of this guideline can be quite difficult.

An unsafe environment greatly decreases the risk taking behaviors required for growth and learning. Only in a safe classroom are students free to fully explore their potential. The teacher has to have discussions with the students about the outcomes of hurtful behaviors and their impact on the other people and the learning environment. This is a sensitizing process. It will take time and consistency to achieve this type of setting. There are certain rules to help attain this, however.

Everyone Is Different, Do Your Best

Poor self-esteem causes many problems in classrooms. Lack of self worth and self-confidence will prevent a child from giving his/her best effort or prevent him or her from trying a task at all. Often, this problem is a result of overt competition in the learning environment setting. Fearing that they will not come up to the standards of the teacher or the other children, some children either don't try their best or don't try at all. By not trying at all or not trying their best, they can always use the excuses that the task was "not that important to them" or "they could do better, but didn't want to." Both of these are face saving techniques. Neither helps children reach their potential.

All people are different. Children develop and learn at different rates. This needs to be understood and respected by teachers. Each child's individuality must be recognized and accounted for in the school setting. To this end, teachers need to remember that a safe place to learn must be a safe place to try new things and a safe place to fail in those trials. Nobody does everything they ever try correctly the first time. Failure or lack of success is not terminal, however. Failure is feedback for subsequent trials. Failure gives us the information we need to refine our efforts so we may succeed at some later point.

Since we all have different learning rates, some children will grasp information and concepts at different times from other children. This is natural and should be treated as such. Problems arise when inappropriate competition is introduced into the classroom as a form of extrinsic motivator. Student efforts are compared and contrasted to other student efforts. Qualitative judgments are made and children are stratified within the class. The "ideal student profile" for that class is established. Some children become the valued ones and others become less valued in this type of setting. It is in such a setting that some children turn off to learning. The mechanisms of learning are not valued in this type of classroom; only the actual learning itself is rewarded. Failure is viewed as inability, rather than feedback. If all the children are to succeed, they need to be respected for their individual worth. The concept of individual differences is one that needs to be addressed in the classroom. Children need to understand that they are all unique and this uniqueness causes differences in learning rates for all people. Sensitivity and patience need to be modeled to students.

Ask for Help When You Need It, Give Help When You Are Asked

If there is respect for individuality in a classroom, this guideline should follow with little difficulty. There has been much work done in the area of cooperative learning. It has been shown to have many strengths. First, it allows all involved to bring their strengths into play in a situation. This expands the possibilities for learning since different people have different experience and knowledge to call upon. Using cooperative learning eliminates inappropriate competition since each person has a responsibility to the learning of the entire group. It provides different approaches to the acquisition of knowledge other than the teacher's. And finally, this approach enhances socialization among participants, increasing the possibilities of mutual and self respect. Since it is acceptable to fail in the quest for knowledge, it must also be acceptable to ask for help in this quest.

Be Honest, Speak Directly

Some people don't realize how difficult this is at times. Using this tact, however, increases meaningful communication and reduces misunderstanding and hurt feelings. Too often, people try to soft pedal what they say in an effort to spare the feelings of the person with whom they are conversing. While this seems considerate on one hand, its can be inconsiderate on the other. If soft pedaling changes the message being delivered, than it increases the possibility of the receiver being hurt later due to inaccurate information about something s/he did or said. When this eventually occurs, which it generally does, the person invariably goes back and asks why the soft peddler didn't tell the truth in the first place.

As the old saying goes, "Honesty is the best policy." We owe this to our students and we need to impress the importance of honesty on our students when dealing with others. Students need to realize that while honesty may hurt in the short term, they are always better off in the long term. Honesty helps students self-actualize and grow. They do not get erroneous ideas about their abilities or performance. Honest feedback and assessment of performance give the best chance for a person to grow since they have a realistic idea of where they are in the process and what they have to do to move forward.

Honesty does not eliminate the need for sensitivity. There are some ways of making honest appraisal easier for the receiver to handle. First, choose words that address the performance or actions, and cannot be misconstrued as an attack of the person. "That answer is incorrect." can sound quite different from, "You're wrong." although many times they are used interchangeably to convey the same message. Explain what you mean and why you say it. Allow the person to ask you questions about your position.

Never use sarcasm. Sarcasm is one the most hurtful forms of indirect communication. If you check the definition of sarcasm in any dictionary, you will find it defined as an aggressive act intended to hurt. As such, it has no place in any meaningful social interaction. Sarcasm stops communication and hurts feelings. If you think back to any times people have been sarcastic with you, you know this is true. You can recognize sarcasm easily. It is generally followed by the statements, "I couldn't help it." or "I just had to say that." The truth of the matter is that they really didn't have to say that, they chose to. The disclaimer usually comes upon the realization they hurt or offended the person they were talking to with the statement.

Children need to practice direct communication. They need to be put in practice situations in which they must find the most effective way to give and accept honest opinions and true constructive criticism. They also need to appreciate honesty in people. While the truth is not always what we want to hear, it is always better in the long run if we do hear it. Honesty is the only shortcut to effective teaching and learning.

Creating a Physically Safe Environment

We can never forget that we are "in loco parentis" of our children. We are legally responsible for their safety while they are in our care. As such it is our duty to protect the welfare and safety of our students when they are with us.

Negligence

Negligence is conduct falling below a responsible standard of conduct established for the protection of individuals against unreasonable harm (NASPE, 1989).

This definition establishes the legal responsibility to act in a prudent manner when we are working with students. There are four components to the concept of negligence. All four must be proven to establish negligence in a court of law.

Duty

If someone is sued for negligence, it must be established that s/he was responsible for the care and safety of the injured party. In other words this person was responsible to act in a prudent manner.

Breech of Duty

Once duty is established, it must be shown that there was a failure to perform this duty. Breech of duty can include acts of commission, doing too much or doing the wrong thing or omission, not doing anything or not doing enough.

Causal Relationship

It must be shown that there was a *close causal relationship* between the failure (breech) to perform the duty and the injury or loss.

Loss or Injury

Finally, there has to actually be some sort of injury or loss that has occurred. If any of these components are not present or can't be proven, negligence cannot be established.

Guarding Against Negligence

There are steps you can take to protect yourself from being negligent. These considerations will not only help you, however, they will also protect your students.

Plan Thoroughly

Safe lessons require planning. Consider the following components when you prepare lessons:

Where Will the Lesson Take Place?

Think of the physical area you will use. Ask yourself the following questions. Is there enough room for the activity I am planning? If not you need to find another site or have to modify activity components to safely conduct the activity in the available space. Changing the locomotor skill; e.g. skipping instead of running, or modifying the equipment being used; e.g., nerf balls instead of playground balls, are ways of doing this. Activities conducted outdoors can be run differently than those conducted in a gymnasium, multi-purpose room or classroom.

Is there any aspect of the site that can cause injury to the participants? Walls (set activity boundaries a safe distance from any walls), columns (these should be padded, if possible), tile floors (these can be slippery and children should never be in stocking feet on a tile floor), fixed hazards or pieces of apparatus (columns or playground equipment), debris (broken glass, litter), temporary hazards (construction equipment, voting booths) all fall into this category. If there are any of these concerns they need to be addressed in the planning of an activity.

What Will the Activity Entail?

What will the students do in the activity? What locomotor form (running, walking, etc.) will be used? Choose a locomotor form appropriate to the size of the area and requirements of the activity. What kind of equipment is being used? Equipment should be the correct size and weight for the person using it. Elementary aged students require equipment that accommodates their size, strength and ability. Certain adult sized equipment is inappropriate at this age level. Broken or questionable equipment should *never* be used. Does the activity require tagging or physical contact? In each case, how children are to touch each other must be explained and demonstrated. If children are working as partners or in small group, children may need to be grouped by size, weight and/or strength. Do the rules of the activity create and maintain a safe environment?

Think about the activity. Is there any way the rules can be interpreted so someone could get injured? If the answer is yes, the rules must be clarified or changed.

Provide Proper Supervision

Keep an eye on your students. There are two ways in which supervision breaks down. The first involves improper supervision. If it is your responsibility to supervise, then you must watch the children. Talking to another person, grading papers or reading prevent you from doing this. Your attention needs to be on the students and what they are doing. This is the only way you can anticipate possible problems or understand what happened if one occurs.

The second way supervision falls short is when there is inadequate supervision. This occurs when there are too many children for the number of supervisors. Both of these situations place children at an increased risk of being injured.

The keys to creating and maintaining a safe learning environment entail your recognizing the physical and emotional needs of the students. Children are individuals just like adults; everyone is unique and has special qualities. People are not for hurting and honesty is the only policy should be remembered. Emotions are fragile characteristics of each individual and none should be compromised in an educational setting. Physical safety requires planning similar to any effective educational setting. Effective planning also ensures your defense against litigation. Keep the best interest of your students in mind at all times and you will remain safe and effective in the learning environment.

Be Prepared in Case of an Injury

Have an emergency procedure in place and review it often. There should be procedures for handling head injuries as well as injuries in which bleeding occurs. With the advent of HIV-AIDS, many schools have instituted required procedures for handling any and all bleeding injuries. Make sure you are familiar with these policies. Have a well-stocked first aid kit handy and know how to use what is in it. Make sure that there is a reporting system in place and fill out all necessary forms if an injury occurs.

Chapter Four

Choosing and Conducting Activities

Chapter Overview

This chapter examines the concept of developmentally appropriate practices and how they are utilized in the selection of activities or games.

Questions to Consider

1. What are Developmentally Appropriate Practices?

2. What needs to be considered when choosing games or activities?

3. How are student abilities considered when choosing appropriate activities?

4. How does the activity level of a game used determine its appropriateness for a particular setting?

There are a number of activities that can be used to help your students learn various cognitive concepts. A number of these activities are included in Chapter 4. However, while there are many of these activities available, the teacher needs to carefully weigh various factors in order to choose those that best suit the needs of the students. This is not as tedious as it sounds as long as you take a few basic things into consideration.

Developmental Appropriateness

Activities you choose must meet the developmental needs and levels of the children with whom you are working. The concept of developmental appropriateness is based on three tenets (Griniski). First, children are not miniature adults. As such, activities you select should not be merely "watered down" adult activities. Second, children develop at different rates. The activities you choose must be adaptable to the differing needs of the various children who will be participating. And finally, today's children will not be adults in today's world. Thus, the concepts and the activities used should prepare students to acquire skills and knowledge they will need in a world that will have progressed beyond our current level.

Ability Level

Choose activities that are appropriate to the physical and cognitive development of the intended audience. The game or activity should be able to be easily understood and easily played by the students. This is particularly important if you want your students to grasp the cognitive concept you are trying to reinforce. This also helps ensure a high amount of participation for each student.

A game or activity may look great on paper, but it may not work in your particular situation. Read the directions for the activity. Will your students easily understand them? If the students are too busy trying to remember intricate sets of instructions or complex movement patterns, they may not be able to concentrate on or understand how the activity teaches them about the content for which you are using the activity. Make sure the activity does not overwhelm the participants. This will be frustrating to you and the students. Activities designed for intermediate level students will probably frustrate primary level students, while primary activities may bore older children.

Activity Level

Make sure the physical activity level is appropriate for the space in which you intend to use it. You can't use an activity designed to be conducted in a gym or on a field in a classroom setting without some modification (See Chapter 5). If you don't intend or don't want to take the time to modify the activity, you may want to choose another. There is a good chance that it will not go well in the alternate setting.

There are several reasons for this. First, there is an increased possibility of injury to the participants. The limited space and large amount of furniture in a classroom makes it unsuitable for an activity requiring a great deal of quick or overt movement. Secondly, it limits the enjoyment of the activity. Large area and fast movement may be a critical component to the design of the particular activity. If this is the case, failure to conduct it in the prescribed matter will lessen the enjoyment of the activity for the participants. This works against the effectiveness of the activity as a learning tool, since the students will lose interest quickly and want to move on to some other activity. Finally, whether you want to or not, you will be forced to modify the activity to make it work in the alternate setting. Since you may not have planned for these alterations, they will take place without a great deal of consideration in a trial and error fashion. The activity will get lost in a sea of new rules. The continuity of the activity will be lost, limiting the learning potential and fun of the activity. It will become a lesson in frustration to all.

Is the Activity Fun?

This is a most important, often forgotten aspect of using activities to present concepts. We sometimes get so caught up with the subject matter, that we fail to keep the atmosphere light and enjoyable. As expected, this creates a setting of drudgery and boredom. The participants, instead of seeing the relationships we are trying to infer, are only wondering when this activity is going to end.

Sometimes the activity is not the problem. Many well-planned activities have failed because of the way in which they were presented. If teachers are going to use this method of teaching, they need to be able to enjoy the activities along with the children. If the teacher can relax and have fun, many times the children can also. This is difficult for some. Some teachers feel that they may lose control of the class or that using games sets a poor example, compromising the perceived importance of the concepts being covered. This does not have to be the case, at all.

Children need to see that teachers are also human. They need to see teachers laugh, problem solve, deal with emotions and interact with others in different settings. This is how children learn about adults and adult behavior. Teachers need to be flexible and genuine.

Equipment Requirements

Check the equipment requirements for the activity you have selected. Do you have the necessary type and amount of equipment? Can you modify or create the types of equipment you need (See Chapter 5)? Is the equipment called for in the activity appropriate to the developmental levels of the children who will be involved in the activity?

If the answer to any of these questions is no, you may want to reconsider the use of this activity. Proper types and sufficient amounts of equipment enhance the participation levels of all the participants of an activity. Sufficient amounts of equipment increases time on task, giving participants a greater number of opportunities to practice and achieve the target objectives of the activity. Proper types of equipment increase academic learning time (ALT) since it provides the appropriate level of difficulty required to make an activity challenging and keep it from becoming too frustrating or boring.

Chapter Five

Activities Across the Curriculum

Chapter Overview

This chapter provides a number of different activities that have been developed to augment curricular content. The chapter is organized by subject area. A list of materials required for each activity is included in the beginning pages.

Questions to Consider

1. What content area will the students be studying?

2. Can I obtain the necessary materials to conduct the activity?

3. Are there any further modifications required to make the activity appropriate for my setting?

Learning Activities

Activities and Equipment Index

All of the activities listed in this index involve the use of a variety of locomotor skills (walking, jogging, running, skipping, hopping, sliding, galloping, etc.) determined by the individual teacher to be appropriate according to the space available and the developmental level of the students involved. Exceptions to the locomotor skills are listed individually and noted by the parentheses following the activity name.

All of the activities are designed to be applicable to either indoor or outdoor facilities. The determination should be made after the teacher has read the **Activity description** *section for the individual activity and selected a locomotor skill applicable to their teaching situation.*

Activity number and title	Equipment required
Geography	
Alphabet Soup (Toss & Catch)	Beachball globes
Around the States	Posters & clue cards
Capital Trash	Scrap paper, pencils, trashcans
Clothespin Capital Tag	Clothespins, cloth U.S. map
Fact Tag	Colored pinnies, alphabet cards
Find It! (Toss & Catch)	Beachball globes
Geography Grab Bag	Puzzle cards of countries and states
Regional Riot	Information cards, hula hoops, signs
Come and Go (Simon Says)	Teacher question list
State What You Know	Pinnies, information cards
Trivia (Toss & Catch)	Variety of balls, question cards
Travel Agency	Question cards
Whose is it? (Toss & Catch)	Variety of balls, state cards, teacher question list
Health	
Did You Catch It?	
Find your food group!	Station & food cards, locomotor skill cards
Floss Frenzy	
Food For Thought	
Food Group Shuttle	Poly spots, food group cards, teacher list
Fruits & Vegetables	Bags, fruits and vegetables cards

(Non-locomotor movements)

Functional Foods
Nutrition Tag
Which am I?   List of fruits and vegetables

Language Arts

Antonym Antics	Antonym, Station & Movement cards
Around the World Vocabulary	Baskets/cans, balls, vocabulary cards
Beachball Spelling	Beachballs, color-coded vocabulary cards
Catch me if you can	Vocabulary cards, cones, polyspots
Compound Partners	Compound word cards
Frantic	Variety of balls, words or concepts cards
Get Together	Statement list, alphabet letter cards
Hoop Scramble	Hula hoops, flag belts, color coded
	Alphabet cards
Inflatable Words	
Knockdown Spelling	
Line 'em Up	
London Bridge	Vocabulary list
Make a "word" game	Alphabet letter cards
Mis-spell Tag	Vocabulary sentence cards
The Mission	Balloons, action cards
Noun Town	Station numbers & cards, action cards
Opposites Attract	Color coded antonym cards
Parachute Spelling	Parachutes & vocabulary lists
"Pick a part..." Tag	Pinnies, sentence cards
Parts Alone	Paper & pencils, flag belts or scarves, color coded cards
Random Rhyming	Color coded rhyming card sets
Sentence Blob Tag	Pencil & paper, pinnies or flag belts, parts of speech cards
Sentence Builders	Paper & pencil, bags, word or phrase cards
Shape Spelling	
Skip & Spell	Vocabulary lists, alphabet cards
Sounds Like	
Spell Check Tag	Pinnies, vocabulary cards
Spelling Unscramble	Color coded alphabet cards
Spelling Word Swing	Color coded vocabulary cards
Story Lines	Word cards, paper & pencils
Story Writers Tag	Clothespins with story related words
Toss n' Spell (Toss & Catch)	Poster boards, vocabulary lists, bean bags
Vocabulary Virus	Pinnies, vocabulary cards
Vowel Search	Vocabulary cards
What did you spell?	Vocabulary lists
Who Am I?	
Wild Card Tag	Flag belts or scarves, alphabet cards

Word Relays   Paper & pencils, hula hoops, alphabet letter
                                               cards

Word Scramble

Life Skills

Add 'em Up
Bodies of Time
Estimation Destination (Walking)   Markers/cones, pathway cards, calculators
Give 'n Take
Human Clock   Number cards for clock face
Musical Months
Recycle Relay
Season's Greetings
Times Up
Tree Sense
Which Way Do We Go?   Directional signs

Mathematics

Balloon Math   Marked balloons
Bizz Buzz   None
Blow Up   Balloons with paper slips
Dog Gone
Freeze Tag   Flash cards, pinnies
Flash Card Frenzy
Guess What!?!   Paper & pencils, cones or markers
The Human Solution   None
Leap Frog   None
Locomotor Finger Throw   None
Math Equation   Number & operation cards
Math Freeze   Equation cards, pinnies
Movement Solutions   None
Number Jumble   Station cards
Number Line   None
Numbers Up! (Toss & Catch)   Variety of bouncing balls
Odds Are Best   Number cards, paper & pencils
Parachute Numbers   Parachutes
Pocket Change
Puzzle Panic   Laminated puzzle cards
Quick Solution Freeze Tag   Pinnies, math sentence cards
Quick Thinking
Relievio   Pinnies, math sentence cards
Shape Up! (nonlocomotor)   Geometric shape cards
Smart Steps   Station number cards
Shape Scramble (nonlocomotor)   Geometric shape cards, rope pieces, bags

Take the money and run   Cones or markers

Miscellaneous

Circle the Circle	Station numbers, question cards
Fact Finders	Color-coded tubes, pinnies, 3X5 fact cards
Get Together	
Hacky Sack	Balloons, beachballs or appropriate balls
Hot Potato (Toss & Catch)	Variety of appropriate balls
Musical Months	Music box, color coded month cards
Olympic Review	Curricular information review cards
Out & Around	Cones or markers
Sequence Scramble	Series of cards
Skip It	Jump ropes

Music

Listen, Watch, Move
Time Travel

Science

Any Old Leaf Will Do	Cones, flag belts or scarves, leaf cards
Earth, Wind, Fire & Water (Toss & Catch)	Variety of balls, list of questions
Ecology Tag	3 hula hoops, flag belts or scarves, pinnies
Fill in the Blank	Alphabet & station cards
Match Tag	Pairs of match cards, pinnies & cones
Now & Then	Pairs of leaf varieties
Orbit Ball	Variety of balls, planet information cards
Planet Scramble	Planet cards
Planet Tag	Planet cards
Polluted Pond	Bean bags and cups
Prehistoric Tag	Dinosaur cards, pinnies
Snakes and Mice	Pencils & paper
Solar System Scramble	Variety of balls

Social Studies

Capture the Revolutionary Flag
Guerrilla Tactics
Presidential Line Up
Take 'em Home
Westward Ho

Geography

Alphabet Soup

Focus: Provide students with an opportunity to utilize knowledge of specific or relative geographic locations.

Summary: Students will utilize their knowledge of world geography to locate the appropriate countries, cities or states according to the criteria described by the teacher.

Success criteria: Students must be familiar with the location of various countries, states and cities around the world that begin with different letters in the alphabet.

Activity diagram: The space required must allow students in pairs or small groups to toss and catch beach ball size globes without interfering with another pair.

Activity description: The teacher will distribute the beach ball type globes that the students will toss back and forth until a designated signal is given. When the signal is given the student who has possession or the one who is about to catch the ball, if it is in the air when the signal is heard, will listen to the directions given. The teacher can have a predetermined list if directions, such as;

-locate a country which name begins with "R",

-locate a state in the United States whose capital begins with "S",

-locate a city whose population is over one million and it begins with "T".

Students can then be responsible for writing down their answer on a sheet of paper. The teacher can use the answers for later discussions. Pairs can work together to solve the more difficult questions.

Equipment required: The teacher may wish to construct a list of appropriate questions prior to the activity or they can simply go from the letter "a" and work to the letter "z" asking for countries, cities or states which begin with the appropriate letter. A globe for each pair is ideal however realistically it can be done in small groups.

Teacher's notes:

Around the States

Focus: Students will move around a specified area using their knowledge of relative positions of geographic locations.

Summary: Students will utilize their knowledge of the states or regions and specific information about each to follow the instructions provided while playing a progressive search game format.

Success criteria: The students will be required to read the information off the cards and be capable of following the directions on the cards.

Activity diagram: The area required can be a large multipurpose room, a gymnasium, or outdoors on a field or playground. The space need only fit the types of loco motor skills incorporated in the activity.

Activity description: Students will be placed in pairs or small groups. The teacher will design and place posters with diagrams of either state or a region of the country (i.e., the Mid-Atlantic states) around the play area. On each poster will be a series of envelopes either numbered or color-coded. Each envelope will contain a clue as to where the student or group of students will go next. These clues could be very easy or could be more difficult depending upon the developmental level of the students and their curricular knowledge base. When they move from one poster to another the clue or directions can give them specific loco-motor skills or types of actions to incorporate while they move to the next poster. Examples would be skipping, wheelbarrow, spider walk, etc. The instructor will regulate the number of posters or stations and the sequence can also be regulated to be terminal or ongoing so that they never finish in the allotted time period.

Equipment requirement: Poster with envelopes and specific clues and information.

Teacher's notes:

Capital Trash

Focus: Specific social studies information is utilized to reinforce student retention and "shooting" at a trashcan is used to entice accurate responses.

Summary: Students will utilize knowledge of the state capitals to answer questions and attempt to score points in a controlled competition.

Success criteria: The material covered in the class lectures; readings and activities must be utilized to answer the questions. The information may be used in both a deductive and an inductive manner.

Activity diagram: This activity may be conducted either in the classroom or in a large open area. The structure of the activity will depend upon the teachers' willingness to allow for movement on the part of the individual students and the class in general.

Activity description: The teacher will decide to either divide the class up into an acceptable number of groups or allow students to work individually. The individual students, pairs, or groups are each given adequate scrap paper and a marker to use to write down their responses to a series of questions concerning the social studies information, i.e. states and capitals. The teacher will ask the individual question and the student, groups or pairs are to write/print their response on the scrap paper and wait for the signal to hold up their responses. Those students holding up the correct response are given one point and instructed to roll up the scrap paper and to shoot at a trashcan or barrel that is placed in an appropriate location. An additional point is given if the student can shoot the trash ball into the can or barrel. The shooter will alternate in each group when a correct response is provided. Originality in the construction of the questions and providing a balance within the groups for the mentally and athletically gifted will provide for more enjoyment on the part of the whole class. You may wish to ensure balanced participation by rotating the students who answer as well as the shooter if pairs or groups are used.

Equipment required: Markers, scrap paper sheets, trashcan or barrel.

Teacher's notes:

Clothespin Capital Tag

Focus: Knowledge of the states and capitals or states and related information are used in a tag game format.

Summary: The students will utilize a clothespin tag game format followed by recall of the location of the states and their corresponding capitals on a large map or information related to individual state, i.e. resources.

Success criteria: The students will need to follow the basic rules for clothespin tag which means no pulling of clothes or holding of an opponent while taking the clothespins, and use their recall of the location of the states and their capitals or specific state related information to complete the task.

Activity diagram: Depending on the size of the students, the teacher can either hang the map of the United States on a wall or they may want to lay it down on the ground in a restricted area. The clothespin tag area must allow for unrestricted movement using a designated loco-motor skill without fear of unnecessary collision.

Activity description: The teacher will divide the class into groups. Each student will be given a portion, four or five, of the one hundred clothespins that correspond to the fifty states and their capitals. These will be attached to their clothes or pinnie on their backs between their shoulder blades. The teacher will designate a specific loco-motor skill to be utilized during the activity. On the teachers' signal the students will attempt to secure as many clothespins from other students [not those in their own group] as possible in the allotted time. When the teacher signals that the clothespin activity is completed they then return to their groups and compare the captured clothespins and determine the locations of the states and the capitals or state related information that they have captured. Each group will then be allowed time to place them on the map in their proper location and if necessary given points for the correct location of clothespins and capitals, bonus points can be given if they have a combination state and capital pair. The activity can then be repeated to attempt to capture any remaining clothespins from players' backs or simply start over and repeat the procedure.

Equipment required: A large map of the United States on which the clothespins can be attached, at least one hundred clothespins with the names of the states and their capitals, different colored pinnies to distinguish the teams if necessary.

Teacher's notes:

Fact Tag

Focus: A tag game format will be utilized to review facts from class curriculum.

Summary: The students will utilize their recall of the facts surrounding specific information covered in curriculum in a tag game format.

Success Criteria: The students will recall information covered in the class and recognize the first letter in the spelling of individual facts.

Activity diagram: The space required will be dependent upon the loco-motor skills incorporated and the size of the class. Generally a large open area that is unobstructed would be considered safe for this type of activity.

Activity description: The teacher will distribute the different colored pinnies for the students to carry. The students will also receive a card with a specific letter on it. This card will be their letter until they tag or are tagged by another student. When the teacher designates a loco-motor skill and the color who will be "It," those students will begin to move around the area tagging students who do not have the same color. When a student is tagged they must provide some fact from the chosen topic (i.e., state capital, resources, city name, etc.) beginning with the letter that "It" is carrying. After they have provided the appropriate fact they exchange letters and colored pinnies with the student and they become the new "It" and begin to chase other colors. This continues until the teacher changes the color of the "Its" and the loco-motor skill.

Equipment required: Enough different colored pinnies for all class members to carry one. Enough alphabet cards for every student to have one to carry.

Teacher's notes:

Find It!

Focus: Student will find specific locations on the globe as they relate to questions from the teacher or partner.

Summary: The students will utilize their ability to locate specific points on a globe according to information provided by the teacher.

Success criteria: The students will be familiar with the locations and corresponding information or clues presented by the teacher during the activity.

Activity diagram: The area must be large enough to allow the students to toss the globes back and forth without causing problems with other pairs performing the same activity.

Activity description: Depending upon the cognitive ability level of the students the teacher will adjust the clues or questions. The students will be asked to gently toss the globes back and forth continuously until the teacher gives some form of signal. On the signal the student who catches the globe will move together with their partner and listen to the clue provided. They will discuss with their partner what they are looking for and manipulate the globe until they can put their finger on the specific location. The teacher will walk around the area providing additional cues and feedback to the pairs.

Equipment required: Enough beach ball type globes for each pair of students to have one and a list of questions or clues to challenge the class.

Teacher's notes:

Geography Grab Bag

Focus: Awareness of locations and relative positioning of states, countries, or other geographic information will be utilized.

Summary: The students will utilize their knowledge of the relative location of countries and states to correctly organize pieces of a geography puzzle.

Success criteria: The students must comprehend the relationship of either countries or states and their position on a map.

Activity diagram: The space required to participate will be dictated by the number of students and the number of countries, states or individual locations utilized in the activity. A large open area or gymnasium will be adequate but a classroom could be used if necessary.

Activity description: The teacher must produce a series of cards that either name a country or state or has a piece of information that pinpoints a specific location on the map relative to the other cards. The students will go to a grab bag and select a card and then proceed to use a loco-motor skill while they communicate and tell each other how to position themselves relative to the remainder of the group as their country, state or specific location would appear on a map of the given area. If the cards are designed with information on both sides then the students can be told to exchange their card with another student, turn the card over and begin to move using the prescribed loco-motor skill to get into a new location relative to the new piece of information. This can continue as they simply switch cards and turn them over each time. The teacher can also hold out one card each time as a central location and the students will have to re-position themselves according to the location of the teacher.

Equipment required: A series of cards with geographic locations or specific information depicting a specific location.

Teacher's notes:

Regional Riot

Focus: Students will incorporate a loco-motor skill and their knowledge of geographic locations in a random movement activity.

Summary: The students will utilize their knowledge of states and their capitals or specific information concerning regions of the United States or continents to form groups according to the information cards they have in their possession on a given signal.

Success criteria: Students must be familiar with the specific information to be utilized in the activity and this should be a review.

Activity diagram: The area should be large enough to accommodate the desired loco-motor skill for the whole class without fear of collision.

Activity description: The teacher will distribute the cards randomly among the class members and ensure that there are additional cards so they can be added throughout the game. Students will be assigned a loco-motor skill with which they may move around the playing area. Players will randomly exchange cards with other students and the teacher throughout the time period. When a signal is given by the teacher the students will move to the correct hula-hoop designated as the area of the country for which their information card pertains and place one foot inside the hoop. The teacher will signal the students to move around again and continue to exchange cards.

Equipment required: Information cards, hula-hoops, sign cards for the areas of the country.

Teacher's notes:

Come and Go [Simon Says]

Focus: Movement among stations that represent position on a map or locations within a specific geographic area.

Summary: Students will utilize specific information concerning relative locations in geography.

Success criteria: Students must understand relative directions of north, south, east and west. Along with this they must understand the concept of relative position.

Activity diagram: An area or space large enough to permit loco-motor movements of students, pairs or small groups without fear of collision.

Activity description: Students can work individually, in pairs or in small groups. Each student, pair or group will be sent to a destination labeled with a specific location such as Colorado, Maine, Florida, etc. There will be two bags or boxes with cards. One box will contain the name of the next location and the other box will contain the name of a loco-motor skill to be utilized while traveling to the next location. Students will choose two new cards at the next station before they drop their cards back into the bags. Each card should have a name of a location on each side or a loco-motor skill on each side.

Equipment required: Sufficient cards will be required to keep the total number of students participating and moving from station to station using a variety of loco-motor skills.

Teacher's notes:

State What You Know

Focus: Curricular material concerning the states will be used to release students in a tag game activity.

Summar:y: The students will utilize their knowledge of the individual states studied in class to provide a fact during the game of tag.

Success criteria: Students will be required to know the information covered in class regarding the states and their important facts.

Activity diagram: The area required will be dependent upon the loco-motor skill selected and the number of students participating in the activity.

Activity description: The teacher will select three or four students to be "taggers" and two of those students will wear the same colored pinnie or T-shirt. These students will be "taggers" and move around the area using the suggested loco-motor skill attempting to tag the other students. When students are tagged they will remain in that spot until one of the "releasers" (wearing another colored pinnie or T-shirt) comes to them to ask a question concerning a state. The "releaser" will have a stack of cards with the information about the states and will ask a question to the player who has been tagged. When they give the correct response they return to the game. If the answer is incorrect the "releaser" will provide the correct answer before moving to the next person. The "releaser" may come back to the student who gave the incorrect response after questioning one other student. They will then ask a different question. The teacher should change the roles of "taggers" and "releasers" often to give all students an opportunity at each role.

Equipment required: A series of 3 X 5 cards with relevant information on them concerning the states. Two different colored pinnies or T-shirts according to the number of students the teacher decides to have as "taggers" or "releasers" at one time.

Teacher's notes:

Travel Agency

Focus: Class formation and collective class knowledge will be utilized to move back and forth across a designated space after answering geography related questions.

Summary: Students will utilize their knowledge and background with specific information surrounding topics in a game format.

Success criteria: Students must be familiar with specific information concerning the states, countries or locations from which the questions are constructed.

Activity diagram: The space required should allow for an area for the students to cross using the specified loco-motor skill and adequate space on either side for the student to stop prior to reaching a permanent boundary.

Activity description: The class will line up on one side of the playing area in a single line. The teacher will utilize a random method to select the first "travel agent" to come to the center and choose a travel location card. The "travel agent" will read the card that will have a statement on it, such as; "You may travel to New York, if you know the state capital." The class will answer in unison. If the answer is correct the travel agent will then read the loco-motor skill on the card and reply, "Skip safely". The students will proceed to "skip" to the opposite side of the playing area without being tagged by the travel agent who must also skip. If they are tagged then they become an additional travel agent for the next question and answer sequence. The first student tagged by the travel agent who read the question then picks a new card and reads the next question. This continues until the students have all been tagged and a new travel agent begins the game again.

Equipment required: A series of cards with specific information written on them along with markers to specify the start and stop lines.

Teacher's notes:

Trivia [Catch and Answer]

Focus: Review of curricular content in a question and answer format.

Summary: Students will utilize information from classroom content of a specific area while tossing and catching an appropriate type of ball or object.

Success criteria: The students are required to be familiar with the curriculum content and also must be capable of reading the cards and answers.

Activity diagram: The area need only be large enough for groups of three students to freely toss and catch an object.

Activity description: Students will form groups of three and the teacher will designate a first student to be the question reader. The first question reader will receive a stack of cards with questions and answers on them from the curricular content being reviewed. The other two students will begin to toss a ball or some other object back and forth until the teacher gives a signal. At that time the student who has the ball, or if the ball is in the air is about to catch the ball, will answer the first question. The student who asks the question will read the question off the card and wait for the answer that is written on the card. If the answering student does not give the correct answer, or any answer, then they provide the correct answer and exchange the stack of cards for the ball and begin tossing with the other partner. The teacher waits until all the groups have resumed tossing and catching before they give the next signal for questions. If one student does not answer a question for three rounds then automatically on the fourth round they receive the next question and switch positions.

Equipment required: Groups of cards with questions and answers on them. These can be done as duplicate series or the groups can exchange their cards after a specific time period. A sufficient number of balls or objects for tossing is required.

Teacher's notes:

Whose Is It?

Focus: A toss and catch ball activity will be used to review geography questions.

Summary: Students will utilize their knowledge of the states and specific information about each one of them to participate in a ball game.

Success criteria: Students will review information concerning each state and then when they participate in the activity they will need to process the information quickly to determine whether it applies to their state.

Activity diagram: An area as small as a shoulder-to-shoulder circle could be appropriate depending upon available room. If the game is played outdoors or in a gymnasium then circle could be larger.

Activity description: Each student in a circle will have a card with the name of a state written on it. On the opposite side of the card will be the information that will be specific to that state: capital, resources, population or any other curricular information available. Each circle will have an identical number of students and they will have the same cards. Therefore, each circle will have a Delaware card, a Maryland card, etc. depending on the number in any one circle. Each circle will also have a ball of some type. Preferably one that bounces easily and high, the teacher will instruct the students that they are to toss the ball in the air at least 10 feet high and it should land in the center of the circle. They may need a little practice with the toss to be somewhat consistent. When they are ready they will all listen to the teacher. The teacher will say toss and then will immediately give a fact from one on the states represented in the circle. The individual student whose state relates to that fact must now attempt to catch the ball before it bounces a second time. Each circle will have one person who should be going for the ball. If two students attempt to catch the ball then the one who is correct will become the next "tosser". The teacher can challenge the students to catch the ball before it bounces or may have to let it bounce two or three times to make the activity appropriate for the age group and the skill level. If catching becomes a problem it may be necessary to simply say touch the ball before it bounces twice and so on.

Equipment required: Enough balls for each group to have one. Enough sets of cards for each group and every student.

Teacher's notes:

Health

Did You Catch It?

Focus: A tag game format is utilized to promote discussions about the spread of illness.

Summary: Students will participate in a tag game designed to simulate the transmission of germs in a classroom or school atmosphere.

Success criteria: Students need only to have appropriate footwear and clothing to participate in a chase and flee activity.

Activity diagram: The students will need an area large enough to utilize the suggested loco-motor skills in an obstacle free environment.

Activity description: The teacher will designate a group of students as "Germs" who will be the chasers in this round of the activity. The Germs will be given a pinnie or some other form of designation to wear. The Germs will also have cards or scarves to give each student which they tag as they move around the area. The teacher will designate the loco-motor skill the students will utilize as they move around the area. Each time the Germs tag a student they will give them one to the cards or scarves. After they have distributed all of their cards or scarves, they return to the teacher for more to distribute. After a specific amount of time or number of cards the teacher will stop the game and discuss with the students how this activity relates to when students are sick and they are distributing their germs around the classroom or school. The students who have more than one card or scarf are at increased risk of catching the flu, cold or virus associated with the cards. Cards can be color coded to match with a specific type of illness. This can lead to discussions about what students can do to minimize the risk of catching the illness. The teacher can also modify the activity and include safe zones as preventative measures which the students bring up in discussion.

Equipment required: The teacher will need some for of designation for the Germs to wear to make it easy to distinguish. The Germs will need to distribute some item such as a card or scarf, etc. as they chase and tag other students.

Teacher's notes:

Find Your Food Group!

Focus: Food pyramid information and loco-motor skill will be used in a random movement activity.

Summary: The students will utilize their experience with the classification of individual foods into the basic nutritional groups in a cooperative group activity.

Success criteria: The students must be familiar with the basic nutritional groups and the classification of individual types of food into their correct grouping.

Activity diagram: The students will be instructed to utilize a loco-motor skill to move around the playing area and this space should be large enough for the students to participate without fear of collision.

Activity description: The teacher will place posters around the designated playing area that will designate the individual nutritional groups that the class has previously studied. In the center of the playing area the teacher will place the cards that contain either a picture or the name of a food or nutritional substance and the designated loco-motor skill on it. When the teacher gives a signal the students will select one card from the pile or bag and decide to which poster it should be taken and read the loco-motor skill to be used in both directions. They will then return to the pile/bag and select another card and repeat the activity. This continues until all the cards have been taken to the posters. The teacher will then lead the class to each poster and check the accuracy of the individual cards. The activity can then be repeated and the class can attempt to set a record for placing the cards at their correct locations in the shortest period of time. This can continue until the teacher is satisfied that the activity has met its' objective or the class has exhausted their enthusiasm.

Equipment required: The teacher will make the posters for the nutritional stations and produce a sufficient number of cards to give each student three, four, five or however many opportunities to place cards at posters.

Teacher's notes:

Floss Frenzy

Focus: Teacher will use a type of flag tag activity to promote discussion concerning the use of dental floss.

Summary: Students will participate in a game where partners attempt to keep the "plaque" players from attacking the tooth students to represent a positive health behavior activity.

Success criteria: Students will understand the concept of cooperative efforts in game activities. They will also possess a basic understanding of the concept of flossing as a healthy dental practice.

Activity diagram: The students will need an area large enough to utilize the suggested loco-motor skills in an obstacle free environment.

Activity description: The teacher will distribute flag belts with two flags to all students. The teacher will designate the loco-motor skill to be utilized. They will then divide the class into four groups and be given a specific colored pinnie to designate what role they will play. One color is the "healthy teeth" that will move around the area freely. One color is the "plaque" students. The last two colors will be the dental floss pairs (one from each color). They will get two ends to a piece of yarn and move around attempting to break the bonds formed by the "plaque" students. A bond is formed when a "plaque" student can steal a flag from one of the "tooth" students. When a flag is stolen then the two students link elbows and move around the area continuing to use the designated loco-motor skill. While the two are moving around the area another "plaque" student can steal the flag from the other side of the "tooth" student. When a "tooth" student has a "plaque" student on each side of them then all three must stand still in the spot where the second student stole the flag. The "floss" students move around in pairs holding on to the ends of the yarn pieces. When they see either two students linked together and still moving using the loco-motor skill or three students standing still then they must get the floss (yarn) between them to break their bond and allow them to return to the game and play some more. Once the bond is broken the "plaque" student who was attached to the "tooth" student may not reattach to the same "tooth" student until they and been attached to at least one different "tooth" student. After a desired time period the teacher should stop the game and change the roles of each color so that all students get to be each of the roles before you debrief the activity and talk about how this related to the discussion of why flossing was an important part of dental health.

Equipment required: 4 different colored pinnines: one for the "plaque" students, one for the teeth, one for the cavity students and one for the dental floss students. Some pieces of yarn about 6' long.

Teacher's notes:

Food for Thought

Focus: Awareness of the classification of food groups is utilized in a question and answer format.

Summary: Students will utilize their knowledge of food groups and individual foods to determine their correct position on the food pyramid.

Success criteria: Students need to understand the concept behind the food pyramid and the individual food groups that make up the levels of the food pyramid.

Activity diagram: Any area in which students can freely move about using a designated loco-motor skill.

Activity description: Each student will be given a card to attach on the back of his or her partner. Once the cards are attached the teacher will designate a loco-motor skill that the students are to utilize to move around the area. On the teachers signal the students find a new partner and show their card to their partner. At that time the partner will give the student on piece of information related to their food (card) and make it in the form of a statement, such as; you are difficult to digest on an empty stomach, you drop from a tree, you are an animal by-product, etc. Then they will ask their partner to give them one fact about themselves. After three or four rounds of partner exchanges students are told to go to designated locations that they believe relate to their position on the food pyramid. Students compare what they have guessed themselves to be with what they actually are and then they receive a new card and find a new partner to begin again.

Equipment required: The teacher must make up cards with pictures or names of specific foods or food groups on them that will attach to the backs of the students. The teacher may also make up posters corresponding to the levels of the food pyramid.

Teacher's notes:

Food Group Shuttle

Focus: Food groups, food pyramid and nutritional information will be required for the students to participate in a tag game format.

Summary: Students will utilize their knowledge of the food groups and nutrients to participate in a tag type of activity.

Success criteria: Students must recognize the different types of food groups and nutrients found in food. These must be easily recognizable from a one-word clue or a small phrase.

Activity diagram: The playing area can consist of either an end-to-end arrangement or a square in which the students must move from one side to the other. The size of the playing area should allow the students to utilize the appropriate loco-motor skills for chasing and fleeing with adequate space for changes of direction without collisions. This will be dependent upon the size of the class or the age of the student participating. Experience will assist the teacher in determining the appropriate area required.

Activity description: Students will be given a food or nutrient group card and be asked to scatter around the area or move to one end, if the playing area is used in only one direction. The teacher will call out an individual food or nutrient group or read a statement from their list and the appropriate group will move to the center and be assigned a loco-motor skill to be utilized by that group when chasing the remaining students. If a student is tagged they then switch cards and become a "tagger". The teacher can call the next group to be the "taggers" and they continue until most or all of the students have been tagged.

Equipment required: Cards with food group names or pictures. The teacher must design a list of various curricular statements for the students to read during the game. Poly spots or markers can be used to designate safe zones or rest areas.

Teacher's notes:

Fruits & Vegetables

Focus: Students will recognize the name of fruits and vegetables and recall the correct spelling of each item.

Summary: Students will utilize their ability to spell the names of fruits and vegetables while participating in a psychomotor activity.

Success criteria: The student should be capable of recognizing and spelling the names of various pieces of fruit and vegetables and recall two distinct movements for vowels and consonants.

Activity diagram: Depending upon the activities chosen for the vowels and consonants this can be conducted in the classroom.

Activity description: The teacher may place the students in small groups of four or five or have the class work together as a whole. S/he will then distribute paper bags to each group with a series of cards or construction paper representations of fruit and vegetables on one side and the correct spelling on the other side. The teacher will then assign a movement for all vowels and all the consonants in the spelling of the name. For example, bend your knees and squat for each vowel and turn around one time for each consonant. The students in each group would take turns putting their hand into the bag and selecting one card or piece of construction paper and announce what they have chosen and then they lead the group in spelling and the corresponding movements for each letter.

Equipment required: Enough paper bags of fruit and vegetable representations to allow all the groups to participate at the same time. Bags can be switched between groups to continue the activity.

Teacher's notes:

Functional Foods

Focus: The food group pyramid will be the basis for a tug-of-war format.

Summary: Students will readily recognize foods and distinguish their position on the food pyramid and utilize this knowledge in a tug-o-war activity.

Success criteria: The students need to be familiar with the designation of the foods used and the correct distribution of food throughout the food pyramid.

Activity diagram: The students will need an area large enough to utilize the suggested loco-motor skills in an obstacle free environment. An additional area with the scooters and rope set up will make the activity move more quickly.

Activity description: The teacher will have enough cards and envelopes for at least two rounds of the activity to start. Each student will be given an envelope with a food card inside. The teacher will designate a loco-motor skill for the students to utilize while moving around the area. Students will randomly meet and exchange envelopes with other students until the teacher signals that they should stop. When they stop moving around the teacher will signal that they can open their envelope and take out the card from the inside. After they see what the food is on their card they move around the area to find individuals that have similar food groups from the food pyramid. The number of cards in each food group should be similar. After all students have found their correct food group the teacher will draw two food groups or food pyramid levels at random to participate in the food group tug-o-war. [If more ropes and scooters are available then additional tug-o-wars can be held.] The students from each of the selected food groups take a position sitting on scooters and grab hold of the tug-o-war rope. When the signal is given the students can only use their feet and legs (they must remain seated on their scooter) to attempt to pull the other team toward them and cause the flag that designates the center of the rope past the cone that designates the tug-o-war zone. Once a team has won the teacher collects the cards in the envelopes and distributes new envelopes for the students to exchange and begin again to prepare for another tug-o-war. This can be repeated as many times as the teacher wants and the teacher can discuss with the students why some food groups are more beneficial for them in physical activities. The teacher should attempt to provide every student the opportunity to participate in at least one tug-o-war.

Equipment required: The teacher will need enough cards with food printed on them and envelopes for the students to exchange. Scooters, a flag to designate the center of the rope, two cones for the tugging zone and a tug-o-war rope

Teacher's notes:

Nutrition Tag

Focus: A review of the food groups will be conducted in a tag game format.

Summary: Student will utilize their ability to distinguish food groups and the major ingredients in foods while participating in a tag game configuration.

Success criteria: Students should be familiar with the food pyramid and the composition of foods that fit each category and approximate portion size.

Activity diagram: The students will need an area large enough to utilize the suggested loco-motor skills in an obstacle free environment.

Activity description: The teacher can designate a loco-motor skill to be utilized and certain students to be the chasers or "diet police." Each of the chasers is given a stack of cards. The chasers pursue the remaining students who attempt to move away. When the chasers are able to tag a student they are presented with a card on which is a food designation. The student who has been tagged must place that card in the appropriate bag or location prior to returning to the game. Once a chaser is out of cards they may either go to the teachers to get more cards or they can become part of the fleers and the teacher can designate a new chaser. After a specific amount of time or at the teacher's discretion the activity stops and the teacher reviews the contents of each bag or box to see how the students have done identifying the foods distributed.

Equipment required: Adequate number of cards to keep the game active for the desired amount of time and signs, boxes or bags for the students to deposit the cards in which correspond to the groups on the food pyramid.

Teacher's notes:

Which Am I?

Focus: Students will use recognition of fruits and vegetables in a run and chase format.

Summary: Students will respond to questions and demonstrate their knowledge of the distinction between fruits and vegetables as called by their correct name.

Success criteria: The students will have discussed and studied the distinction between various types of fruits and vegetables and will know them by their correct names and classifications.

Activity diagram: The space required will need to be large enough to provide sufficient room for a chase type activity without the fear of collisions. The number and age of the students will also make a difference.

Activity description: The teacher will allow the students to pick a partner that they feel comfortable with for the activity. Normally a student of comparable speed will be best. The teacher will designate a centerline for the activity and then two end lines that are far enough from the closest wall or boundary to provide sufficient space for the students to stop from a full sprint. The pair of students will line up at the centerline a comfortable distance apart. Students may pick their own distance to provide the pairs with individual challenge. The teacher will designate one side to be fruit and the other side as vegetables. The teacher will tell the students to be ready for the next word that will be either a fruit or a vegetable. When the word is called whichever it is, a fruit or a vegetable, that group will chase the other group and attempt to tag them before they cross the end line. If they are successful at tagging them then they switch sides, if not they remain on the same side. This will be repeated with the teacher randomly selecting fruits and vegetables. The teacher should also let the students change partners periodically to keep them interested. The loco-motor skill used to chase can also be changed to provide variety to the activity.

Equipment required: A space large enough to allow the students to run or use whatever loco-motor skill the teacher decides. A list of fruits and vegetables with which the students will be familiar should be written. Clothing or some other means to designate chasers.

Teacher's notes:

Language Arts

Antonym Antics

Focus: Knowledge of antonyms and their definitions are used in a partner matching activity.

Summary: The students will reinforce their knowledge of antonyms in a game setting.

Success criteria: The students must be familiar with the antonyms and their definitions that are utilized as well as the loco-motor skills assigned.

Activity diagram: The area required must allow for the free movement of students using the assigned loco-motor skill without obstruction or fear of collision.

Activity description: The students will be given a card at random with either a word or it's definition on it. The teacher will select a loco-motor skill that the students will utilize to move around the area. Students will move through the center of the area and look for their match among all the other students. If they do not find their match then they continue to use the loco-motor skill and pass around one of the corner cones before returning to the center area to look again. When two students have found their match they go to the teacher to get another card and return to the center area. The teacher will have enough cards to keep the partners returning to the center area for the desired amount of time.

Equipment required: The desired number of cards with either the word or the definition of the word in pairs. Four cones or makers are needed for the corners around which the students travel while using the designated loco-motor skill.

Teacher's notes:

Around the World Vocabulary

Focus: Students will use basketball shots as a reward while reviewing vocabulary words.

Summary: Students will cooperate with a partner to review vocabulary word spelling and definitions.

Success criteria: The students must be familiar with all the words and definitions included in the vocabulary review.

Activity diagram: The teacher will determine the appropriate set up for the activity. This could be a plastic trashcan representing a basketball basket or a box that would represent a soccer goal. These would be spaced far enough apart so that groups of students working at one basket or goal will not interfere with an adjacent basket or goal. Small soft sponge balls should be used for shooting.

Activity description: Around the basket or goal the teacher will mark five spots from which the student will shoot. One partner will stand at the spot designated as their first choice and will be ready to shoot. First they must correctly spell the vocabulary word that is first on their list. If they are correct they shoot. If they are incorrect they must repeat the correct spelling before they shoot. If they miss the shot they must give the correct definition before a second attempt. If they do not know the correct definition their partner will read it and they repeat it before they go to the next spot to shoot from and repeat the process. After they have shot from all five spots they switch roles with their partner. Each partner should have a list with the vocabulary words listed in different sequence so the first shooter is not always at a disadvantage.

Equipment required: The teacher will need at least two different copies of the vocabulary list, one for each partner. As many as two or three pairs could work at one basket or goal. Consequently the teacher will need to determine the appropriate number of required baskets/goals.

Teacher's notes:

Beach Ball Spelling

Focus: Review of spelling and vocabulary words.

Summary: The students will utilize their knowledge of vocabulary words in a spelling activity while performing a loco-motor skill.

Success criteria: The students must be familiar with the vocabulary words listed on the cards. They must also be capable of performing all the loco-motor skills utilized on the beach balls.

Activity diagram: The space required will be limited to the number of groups and beach balls that the teacher designates.

Activity description: Groups of three will work together with two of the three passing a beach ball back and forth while the third holds a group of cards. When the teacher gives a signal the student who has the ball or catches the ball if it is in the air, looks at one of their thumbs and call out the color of the panel on which the thumb is resting. The third member of the group looks at the card and reads the word listed next to that color. The student then spells the word correctly or has it spelled correctly for them and then exchanges the ball for the stack of cards. The pattern continues with tossing and catching and spelling of words on the teachers' signal. If one student does not get a turn to spell after three rounds then they should automatically be included.

Equipment required: Beach balls with colored panels. Series of cards with color-coded vocabulary words listed on them.

Teacher's notes:

Catch Me If You Can

Focus: The student vocabulary list will be the vehicle for a chase and flee activity.

Summary: Students will utilize their knowledge of their vocabulary list and the correct spelling of each of the words in a chase and flee activity.

Success criteria: The teacher will lead the class in writing their vocabulary words on individual cards (small cardboard cards). Each student will have their own set of vocabulary cards to carry with them during the activity.

Activity diagram: The area used must be large enough for the students to safely move around using the selected loco-motor skill without fear of collision. In many cases more than half the class will be moving at the same time. Boundaries or safe spots/zones can be set up to allow the students to have an terminal point to their chases.

Activity description: Each student will have a series of cards with the individual vocabulary words correctly spelled on them. The teacher will have the students find a partner and spread out inside the playing area. One student will be selected to be the speller and the other will be the chaser. The teacher will assign a loco-motor skill for the spellers and chasers to use and this can be changed at any time during the activity. The speller will stand behind the chaser and begin to spell the vocabulary word on the top of their card pile by touching the chaser on alternating shoulders for each letter. (Example: Touch left shoulder...D, touch the right shoulder...O, touch the left shoulder...G.) When the chaser hears the last letter they must shout out the vocabulary word and then turn around and attempt to chase the speller using the assigned loco-motor skill and touch the speller before they get outside the boundaries or to a safe spot/zone. If the speller is successful at reaching a safe zone/spot they go to a new chaser and select a new word. If they are tagged then they take a position as a chaser and wait for someone to come and begin spelling by touching their shoulders. This continues with spellers and chasers changing roles and words for as long as the teacher is satisfied with the results of the activity.

Equipment required: Small pieces of cardboard for the vocabulary words. Markers are used for the boundaries and poly-spots for safe zones/spots.

Teacher's notes:

Compound Partners

Focus: Compound words are incorporated with loco-motors skills in a random movement activity.

Summary: The students will utilize their experience with compound words to locate appropriate partners and perform a loco-motor skill in unison.

Success criteria: Students will recall their preparation with compound words and the use of loco-motor skills while they search for appropriate partners in the class activity.

Activity diagram: The space required will be determined by the number of students and the designated loco-motor skills to be utilized. The space should be adequate for movement without fear of collisions.

Activity description: The students will each receive a card that they will conceal until the activity begins and then they will hold it in front of their chest as they move around the playing area. The teacher will designate two loco-motor skills: one which will be used by the students as they move around the area looking at other students' words and the second loco-motor skill which they utilize with their compound word partner as they change loco-motor skills and attempt to move in unison. When student have been together a sufficient period of time, maybe one lap around the perimeter, then they return to the teacher to receive a new card and repeat the process.

Equipment required: The teacher will make up enough cards for the students each to have one and then have enough to handout the extras as they complete one round of the activity. Words that have more than one match are most appropriate: snowman, snowball, snowfall, bedroom, bathroom, etc.

Teacher's notes:

Frantic

Focus: Toss and catch activity utilized to review vocabulary word lists.

Summary: Students will utilize their ability to spell vocabulary words or associate concepts in an eye hand coordination activity.

Success criteria: Students must be capable of spelling vocabulary words and cooperatively participating in a sequence activity.

Activity diagram: The area needed will be determined by the students' ability to pass and catch. The number of individual groups and the size of the object being passed will also be determining factors.

Activity description: The teacher will put the students into groups to work together. The size of the groups may vary. The larger the number of students in each group then the fewer the opportunities to participate. Students will practice receiving the ball from the one person and throwing or tossing it to the next person in the same sequence each time. Once this pattern is established they maintain it until the teacher asks them to change it. Each pass and catch will represent one item or letter in the sequence. The teacher will give the directions for the total number of passes and catches to be made by the group. Sample commands could be:

    Spell cat,
    Spell the name of our state,
    What are the four seasons?
    What are the vowels, etc.?

These tasks can be modified to meet the level of the student's capabilities. This activity could easily be modified to incorporate into a math class.

Equipment required: Balls that the students are capable of manipulating safely and effectively. A list of curricular statements, words or concepts from class notes to use as samples.

Teacher's notes:

Get Together

Focus: Review of vocabulary words is accomplished by using individual letters that make up common words.

Summary: Students will utilize their recall of the correct spelling of vocabulary words to create words from individual letters working cooperatively.

Success criteria: Knowledge of the vocabulary list and the correct spelling of the words prior to participating. Students must be capable of working cooperatively to solve problems and interact to achieve a common goal.

Activity diagram: Sufficient space will be required for the class to move around as individuals and then in small groups without coming in contact with others. The teacher may choose different loco-motor skills that increase or limit the movement of the students according to their energy levels.

Activity description: The students will be given a card that has letters on both sides. They will also be told what combination of loco-motor skills to utilize. Any finally they will be given the clue:
· Create a word with three letters
· Create a word that makes you think of spring
· Create a word that has a double consonant
· Create a word that is an antonym, etc.
Students will also be told how to move around the area skipping, sliding, etc. until they have found others who will form the solution to the problem and then skip, slide, gallop, etc. together as a group until they hear the next clue. Then break up and find a new group. If students cannot find suitable group members to satisfy the clue they may go to the letter stockpile and select a suitable letter and then join their group.

Equipment required: Laminated letter cards with different letters on each side. There must be at least twice the number of cards as students in the class. The distribution of the letters should reflect the variety of words on the students' vocabulary list. Pay close attention to individual consonants used in your vocabulary list.

Teacher's notes:

Hoop Scramble

*Focus***:** Vocabulary and spelling will be used in conjunction with a chase and flee team activity.

Summary: Students will use their ability to spell and compose words from mixed letters secured in a game that requires agility.

Success criteria: The students will use all their existing vocabulary to devise words in a scrabble type configuration; i.e., up or down, to score points for their team.

Activity diagram: The size of the required area will depend upon the number of students and the loco-motor skill utilized.

Activity description: The class will be divided into four even teams. Each student will secure one flag representing his or her team color. The teacher will distribute four hula-hoops around the playing area and they will represent each team color. The students will move to their team's hoop. When the teacher tells the students to begin they will use the prescribed loco-motor skill and attempt to secure as many alphabet cards from the other teams hoops as possible in the allotted time period. They may only take one card at a time from another team's hoop before returning it to their hoop. If they have a card in their possession, an opponent may steal their flag. If a player has their flag stolen they must exchange the letter in their possession for the return of their flag before returning to the activity. Therefore, if a player has an alphabet card in their possession they may not steal anyone else's flag until they have returned it to their team's hoop. Once the time period has elapsed a team may only use captured alphabet cards (colors other than their own) to compose as many words as possible for team points.

Equipment required: Four equivalent sets of different colored alphabet cards with enough letters to make several words corresponding to the general class vocabulary or spelling list. Enough flags or strips of clothe, preferably of four different colors, for each student to have one and four different colored hula-hoops.

Teachers' notes:

Inflatable Words

Focus: Recognition of spelling and vocabulary words will allow students to participate in a parachute activity.

Summary: Students will incorporate vocabulary lists and parachute activities to review word spelling and meanings while performing with a parachute.

Success criteria: Students must know the word spelling meaning in order to participate appropriately.

Activity diagram: Depending on the size of the class more than one parachute may be necessary. There should be an adequate number of students around each parachute so that regardless of the word that is used there will still be enough students to properly perform the functions with the parachute.

Activity description: Students will be randomly given letters that are part of the words listed on their vocabulary or spelling lists. Each student will then take a position around the outer edge of the parachute and have both hands on the edge in order to raise and lower the parachute in the typical fashion. The teacher will give the command to raise and/or lower the parachute. When the teacher asks the students to raise the parachute they will pause for a second and then either call out a word or read a definition of the word. When the students hear a word which contains the letter which they have been assigned they will run under the parachute and either spell the word aloud or recite the definition of the word depending on the instructions of the teacher at the beginning of the activity. As soon as they have finished completing the assigned task they return to the outer edge of the parachute and await the next command to raise the parachute and the next word. The teacher should attempt to ensure that each student goes under the parachute a similar number of times utilizing their individual letter.

Equipment required: The number of parachutes will depend on the size of the class and the length of the words on the vocabulary list. Students not going under the parachute must be able to control the parachute while their classmates are underneath the inflated parachute.

Teachers' notes:

Knock Down Spelling

Focus: Students will spell words from retrieved letters using a bowling type activity.

Summary: Students will utilize vocabulary words as the scoring for a bowling competition using bowling pins and nerf or sponge balls.

Success criteria: Students should have knowledge of and the ability to spell a variety of words from the suggested list and from memory.

Activity diagram: Activity can be performed against the walls or by having a large enough area for two groups of students to be facing one another when they are rolling the balls at the target pins.

Activity description: Bowling pins (or some suitable substitute) will be positioned either against a wall of in the center of an area where students can roll the provided balls at the pins. Under or behind each pin should be a stack of letter cards (approximately five for each pin would be sufficient) from which the students can retrieve a single card when they knock down a pin. After they knock down a pin they should run out to retrieve one letter card and then stand the pin back up again for the subsequent attempts by their teammates. After a specific time period or number of throws the teacher stops the rolling and the students take all the letter cards which they have retrieved and utilizes them to spell as many words from their vocabulary list as possible. The teacher may have some bonus letters or some letters that are designated as wild card or free letters. Once a round is over the students distribute the letters again to the individual pins for the next round and the activity begins again with the same or a different list.

Equipment required: Sufficient number of pins and letters depending on the number of students participating in each round or activity.

Teacher's notes:

Line 'em Up

Focus: Letter sequencing or the alphabet will be reviewed as a consequence of this random loco-motor skill activity.

Summary: Students will recall the correct sequence for either the alphabet or numbers according to they card they have in their possession.

Success criteria: The students will need experience and knowledge of sequencing of letters of the alphabet or numbers and denominations.

Activity diagram: Students need an area adequate to utilize the suggested loco-motor skill free of obstacles and dangerous obstructions around the perimeter

Activity description: Each student will receive one card. On the signal the students will begin to move around the designated area using the designated the desired loco-motor skill with a card in their hand. There will be cones placed on the outer boundaries of the area and each time the students exchange a card with another student they must use the designated loco-motor skill to go around one of the cones before they exchange with another student. They may not go around the same cone again until they have been around all of the other cones. After the desired period of time the teacher will signal for the students to stop and get in their proper sequence according to the card they have at the time the teacher stopped them. This can be repeated as many times as the teacher feels appropriate. This same activity can be done with letters, words, numbers or monetary denominations.

Equipment required: Teacher must provide a series of cards for the students to carry and exchange.

Teacher's notes:

London Bridge

Focus: Vocabulary and spelling words are the focus of a group activity to review these skills.

Summary: Students will use vocabulary words to engage in a game that requires the recall of the correct spelling of individual words.

Success criteria: The students need only to recall the spelling of their vocabulary words to participate in this activity.

Activity diagram: The class will need adequate room for them to perform a desired loco-motor skill and stop whenever they move to forming a new bridge.

Activity description: Pairs of children are placed randomly around the playing area. When the teacher gives the signal the students will begin to use the assigned loco-motor skill to move around the area. The teacher will then call out a letter and tell the students to think of a word either which begins with that letter or a word which has that particular letter in the spelling somewhere. When the students are able to think of and spell a word that meets the teachers' specifications they then move on a given signal to find a partner. This need not be their original partner. This pair holds their joined hands up in the air. The first student then spells the word they have chosen. If it is correct then the second student spells their word. If either is incorrect, then they request the correct spelling from the teacher or another pair of students. The teacher can change the letter and the loco-motor skill at any time during the activity.

Equipment required: Vocabulary list

Teachers' notes:

Make a "Word" Game

Focus: A scrabble type game used in a cooperative format among students.

Summary: Students will demonstrate their knowledge of the different classifications of words and their correct spelling in a game format.

SuccesscCriteria: The students will be capable of differentiating between the various classifications of words and also utilize correct spelling of their vocabulary words.

Activity diagram: The students will be required to move around the area using various loco-motor skills during each activity. The space required will depend on the number and size of the students and the loco-motor skills utilized.

Activity description: The teacher will provide each student with one card with a letter of the alphabet on it. The teacher will then suggest the loco-motor skill to be utilized. The students will listen for the type of word, i.e., proper noun, verb, pronoun, etc. which they are to form. They should begin to move around the room holding up their letter using the loco-motor skill and attempt to move together with other students who will form a word that fits the suggested classification. If they are unable to use their letter or if they find a group of students looking for a specific letter to complete a word, they may return to the letter stockpile and select another appropriate letter. If a word is completed then that group is to return to the stockpile and get new letters and continue the loco-motor skill until the teacher changes the task and the loco-motor skill. The teacher can use either a time limit or an arbitrary period before changing the classification. The secret is to not let the students become bored or frustrated.

Equipment required: The teacher must produce enough letters to provide adequate opportunity for students to be successful. This means multiple sets of common letters, e.g. vowels.

Teachers' notes:

Misspell Tag

Focus: A chase and flee activity used for the review of spelling or vocabulary words.

Summary: The students will participate in a tag game activity where they will use their ability to correctly spell vocabulary words.

Success criteria: The students must be familiar with their vocabulary list and the correct spelling of the words on that list. They must also be familiar with the usage of the words in sentences.

Activity diagram: The space required must accommodate the freedom of movement in a chase and flee type activity without fear of collision using a designated loco-motor skill.

Activity description: The teacher will randomly designate a group of students to be the "taggers" at the beginning of the activity. Each of these students will carry a designation for being the "tagger" (hat, pinnie, etc.) and a card with a sentence on it. When the "tagger" has successfully tagged one of the other students then that student will read the sentence on the card, identify the misspelled word and correctly spell the word. If the word is misspelled again they will be given additional chances to correctly spell the word. After a series of attempts the "tagger" will look at the opposite side of the card for the correct spelling and recite it to the student. After this has occurred the "tagger" will give his card and the taggers' designation to the student. The new "tagger" will go to the teacher for another card and then return to the activity to tag another student and repeat the process.

Equipment required: Cards with the vocabulary words misspelled in sentences and the correct spelling on the opposite side of the card. T-shirts, hats, pinnies, etc. to act as designations for the "taggers."

Teachers' notes:

The Mission

Focus: Students will utilize common and familiar Spanish words written on cards in a movement activity.

Summary: The students will utilize their bilingual skills to complete activities that are described with a combination of English and Spanish descriptors while cooperating with their partners.

Success criteria: The students will be responsible for the recall of specific vocabulary words written in Spanish and then demonstrate their ability to perform actions and activities required to complete the task.

Activity diagram: The activity will require that students to work in pairs and cooperate to complete a series of tasks using a variety of activities and actions. The space required should allow for freedom of movement by the students as they use specified loco-motor skills.

Activity description: The teacher will prepare a series of cards which describe activities such as, moving along a line on the floor, moving around a cone, moving from the intersection of two lines to the next intersection of two lines, moving to a wall, etc. and they will prepare a second set of cards which describe the actions the students must perform to complete the tasks such as, skipping, hopping, sliding, walking like an ostrich, etc. Each of these series of cards will be place either in a bag or face down on the floor in a specific area or location. On each of the cards specific words used to describe the activity or action should be written in Spanish. Students will have studied the Spanish words in their vocabulary lists and understand how to complete the tasks and actions according to the directions. The students will select a partner to complete the series of tasks selected at random on each round. One partner will be designated to begin the round. They will use a designated loco-motor skill to move to the first bag or area of cards and then move to the second area or bag to select an action card to complete the task. After they complete one task they will switch roles with their partner. While the first partner is completing the task the second partner will be given a balloon to keep in the air by continuously tapping it with their hands, feet, arms, legs, or head. When the first partner completes their task and returns to home base they exchange the balloon responsibility without catching it or letting it hit the floor. When the second partner completes their first task they return and again switch the balloon responsibility. This switching of roles continues until the teacher decides to halt the process. Students who have trouble with the Spanish vocabulary may ask a fellow student or the teacher for assistance.

Equipment required: Enough cards for the students to continually be choosing new and different tasks and actions in pairs. Depending upon the tasks set up by the teacher various markers may be necessary according to the area or location.

Teachers' notes:

Noun Town

Focus: Students use reading skill and loco-motor movement skills to move around a designated area.

Summary: Students will utilize various forms of locomotion to negotiate the stations in the activity without contacting other students.

Success criteria: The students must be capable of reading the cards and posters and performing the activities described on the cards.

Activity diagram: The space required will be need to be large enough to allow for freedom of movement by all the students at the same time in different directions without fear of collision.

Activity description: The posters of the individual locations such as, the mall, the grocery store, car wash, etc. will be place around the playing area. Underneath each poster will be two bags of cards. One bag will contain the names of the other locations designated on the posters and the other bag will contain cards with verbs, animals, loco-motor skills, actions or any other type of movement classifications that the teacher would like to utilize. The first bag tells the student where to go and the second bag tells them what to do to get there. The students will continue from station to station until the teacher decides to stop the activity or the students visited a specific number of locations. Students can be given checklist sheets to see how often they visit each location or if they have visited all the locations.

Equipment required: Posters with the names of locations on them and the corresponding groupings of cards for the bags. Additionally the cards that describe the actions or movements to get to the next station will also be necessary.

Teacher's notes:

Opposites Attract

Focus: Word recognition is used to find partners as they match-up antonyms while performing loco-motor skills.

Summary: Students will utilize their knowledge of antonyms to pair words according to their meanings.

Success criteria: Students must be capable of distinguishing the opposite for a series of words commonly used in their vocabulary lists.

Activity diagram: The space required should allow for the movement of the students utilizing the prescribed loco-motor skill without fear of collision.

Activity description: The teacher will distribute laminated cards that are color coded to enable the teacher to assign the role of chaser according to the color of the cards in the student's possession. When the teacher calls out the color of the cards that will be "chasers" they attempt to tag any other students and then exchange cards with them. The new "chaser" attempts to tag someone else until the teacher changes the color of the "chasers'" cards. On a predetermined signal the students must partner up with their antonym partner and then the game becomes a partner tag game. This can go back and forth from singles to partners on the decision of the teachers as many times as the activity warrants.

Equipment required: Pairs or series of antonyms printed on laminated color-coded cards.

Teacher's notes:

Parachute Spelling

Focus: Students will use letter recognition and spelling word lists to participate in a parachute play activity.

Summary: Students will use short-term memory to retain a letter of the alphabet and utilize their knowledge of spelling and vocabulary to respond to words using their assigned letter called by the teacher.

Success criteria: Students must have a working knowledge of the vocabulary list and the correct spelling of the words to enable them to respond quickly as the teacher calls out the words while the parachute is being raised and lowered.

Activity diagram: Adequate room must be available to allow for the circumference of the parachute when completely open as well as room around the outside for students to stand and move freely.

Activity description: Students will be assigned a letter of the alphabet and then take a position around the perimeter of the parachute or multiple parachutes depending upon the size of the class, number of parachutes available and the space available. When the teacher is ready the children will be instructed to pick up the parachute with both hands and hold it at waist level. The teacher will now call out a vocabulary word and tell the students to raise the parachute. If the word begins with the child's assigned letter or is contained in the vocabulary word they are told to run under the parachute while it is billowing up and return to their spot before the class lowers the parachute to their waist again. The teacher should also make certain that the letters are used randomly and comprehensively so that no child is standing and waiting too long between turns. The time when the words are called can be adjusted according to the ability level of the class (the teacher can call the words as the parachute is going up, or when it is at its height, etc.) to make the children think and respond more quickly.

Equipment required: One or more parachutes and the class vocabulary list.

Teacher's notes:

"Pick a Part..." Tag

Focus: Using a chase and flee activity students will review their knowledge of the parts of speech in a sentence.

Summary: The students will be capable of identifying the individual parts of speech associated with words in a sentence.

Success criteria: Students must be capable of identifying the parts of speech used in sentence structure when they hear a given word used in a complete sentence.

Activity diagram: The students must have sufficient space to participate in a chase and flee type activity using the designated loco-motor skill without fear of collision.

Activity description: The teacher will designate a specific loco-motor skill to be used by the students in this chase and flee activity. The teacher will select a group of students to be "chasers" initially. Each of the "chasers" will be given a colored pinnie and a card with a sentence written on it. They will attempt to tag a student and read the sentence on the card. They will ask the student to identify the part of speech for a specific word in the sentence. They will begin with the first word in the sentence and as they tag each subsequent student they will use the next word in the sentence. If a student is incorrect they will provide the correct answer before chasing the next student. Once they have gotten to the last word in the sentence on their card they will give their pinnie and their card to that student after they attempted to identify the part of speech correctly. That student will then take the card to the teacher to exchange it for another sentence and begin to chase members of the class.

Equipment required: The teacher must make up sufficient cards with sentences to prevent the reuse of sentences too frequently. Colored pinnies for the "chasers."

Teacher's notes:

Parts Alone

Focus: Scarf tag is used to review the concept of parts of speech and sentence structure.

Summary: Students will differentiate the parts of speech and construct complete sentences using a team game approach.

Success criteria: Students will practice differentiating the parts of speech (nouns, verbs, pronouns, etc.) in the classroom. They will also understand how to utilize them in complete sentences.

Activity diagram: A large open area will be needed where the players can run and change direction. The number of students and the age will dictate how much space will be needed. The ideal surface would be a large grass covered area. The area will be broken down into sections for each of the parts of speech to use as their home base.

Activity description: Students will be randomly assigned to groups. Each player will take two scarves to tuck into their pants. To identify each group they will wear different colored tops. Cards for the various parts of speech will be color coded cards, i.e. red for nouns, blue for verbs, green for adverbs, etc. Each player will begin with four random cards. When the teacher gives the signal the students will attempt to capture the scarves of other group members. Each time they capture a players' scarf that player must give them one of their cards. They get their scarf back and put it back into their pants waistband and return to play. Any time two players are exchanging scarves for word cards they may not have their scarves stolen. When the teacher gives the signal the groups go back to their area and get together to see how many different parts of speech they have captured and then they attempt to construct sentences using the words that represent the cards. They will write the sentence down and count how many of the cards they use and receive one point for each card used. This can then be followed by discussion of the sentences each group has constructed.

Equipment required: Flag belts or enough scarves for each player to have two (scarves can be twelve inch strips of white sheet or some other rag torn up). Colored cards to correspond to the types of words, there should be enough for each player to have at least four cards to start and then they may come back to the teacher when needed to get more before they return to the game. Students will need paper and pencils to write down their sentences at the end of the game. Different colored tops for the individual groups.

Teacher's notes:

Random Rhyming

Focus: A crossover pattern and a tag game format will be incorporated to review the concept of rhyming words.

Summary: Students will demonstrate their knowledge of the concept of rhyming in a tag game activity.

Success criteria: The students will practice the concept of selecting words that are similar in sound and possibly structure and be capable of reading these words from a series of flash cards prior to participating in this activity.

Activity diagram: The area required for this activity should have flat surfaces at each end (possibly portable blackboards which are clean). The area must be large enough to permit a chase and flee type of tag game. The students should be instructed to use loco-motor skills that restrict their speed and change of direction.

Activity description: Students will receive one card with a word written on it to begin. Each card must have a type of adhesive mechanism (scotch tape, Velcro, etc.) on it. The teacher will select approximately one quarter of the students to be the "taggers" initially. The players who are designated as "taggers" should stand in the center of the playing area. The remainder of the class is told to separate and move behind the lines at either end of the playing area. On the teachers command students will attempt to cross the playing area using a designated loco-motor skill and get to the other end without being tagged. If they are tagged, they present their card to their "tagger" and stay in the center to tag other students. If they are successful at crossing the area without being tagged then they go to the wall or blackboard and exchange their card for one that rhymes. They then return to the line and attempt to cross again.

Equipment required: Sets of flash cards with rhyming words on them. Adhesive tape or some other type of adhesive mechanism is used to hold the cards on the blackboard.

Teacher's notes:

Sentence Blob Tag

Focus: The students will construct sentences from random parts of speech using a tag activity.

Summary: Students will participate in a cooperative tag type activity and utilize their ability to follow directions to build sentences when the activity is complete.

Success criteria: The students will recognize and understand the usage for the various parts of speech used in constructing sentences.

Activity diagram: The space required should allow for the unobstructed movement of the students using the designated loco-motor skills.

Activity description: Each student will be given a laminated color coded card with a part of speech printed on it or a pinnie or flag belt which color corresponds to a part of speech; such as, noun, article, preposition, etc. A group of students will be determined to be "taggers" for the first round. Those students who are "taggers" will move around the area using the designated loco-motor skill to tag the remainder of the class. Each time they tag someone that person must link elbows or hold hands with the individual who tagged them. As that pair tag another student they too link elbows or hold hands with the group. This cooperative effort to tag students continues until all of the individual students have become part of the groups moving as "taggers". At this time students will work in their groups to construct sentences using all the parts of speech that make up their group of "taggers". They can be given pieces of paper to write their sentences down, come up to a blackboard to write their sentence, or simply stand in line in the correct order and recite their sentence for the remainder of the class. The teacher may place or remove restrictions as to whether the students may use additional words or be restricted only to words that made up their blob group at the end of the tag activity. The teacher should have additional cards and exchange them with the students and select a new group of students to be "taggers", designate the loco-motor skill and start the activity again.

Equipment required: Pinnies, flag belts or laminated color-coded cards with the parts of speech printed on them, pencils and paper to write sentences on, if desired.

Teacher's notes:

Sentence Builders

Focus: Using collected cards to designate parts of speech students will review sentence construction.

Summary: The students will construct sentences using various types of word classifications or phrases to devise a complete thought.

Success criteria: The student must understand each of the word classifications and phrases utilized in this activity in order to construct sentences that represent complete thoughts.

Activity diagram: The space required must allow the students, in pairs, to move around freely utilizing loco-motor skills assigned by the teacher.

Activity description: The students will be asked to find a partner. The pairs will be given a piece of paper and a pencil or pen. The teacher will place paper bags randomly around the playing area. Inside each paper bag will be a group of cards with either words (noun, pronoun, verb, etc.) or a phrase (prepositional phrase, adverbial phrase, etc.) on each one. The pair will be told to begin with two words: a noun and a verb. They will then move around the room collecting cards from the bags using the assigned loco-motor skill until they have five cards. They will then stop and construct a complete sentence using the five cards and the two words with which they began. They will each write down their sentence on their individual piece of paper. The students will then replace their cards in various paper bags. They will select a new partner and repeat the activity. After this has taken place a number of times the teacher will ask for volunteers to share some of their sentences.

Equipment required: Paper bags and word or phrase cards for each bag.

Teacher's notes:

Shape Spelling

Focus: Review of vocabulary or spelling words in a random movement format.

Summary: Students will recall the spelling of words that correspond to the shape designated by the teacher in a random fashion.

Success criteria: Students must be familiar with the selection of words chosen by the teacher for this activity. The proper spelling is a review of previously covered vocabulary words.

Activity diagram: Students need an area adequate to utilize the suggested loco-motor skill free of obstacles and dangerous obstructions around the perimeter.

Activity description: The teacher will distribute cards to each student. The format of the activity should be random movement around the area using a prescribed loco-motor skill. On the signal given by the teacher the students should partner up at random. When all students have found a partner the teacher will call out a shape. The students will decide who will go first between the two of them. When the first student is ready they will read the word that corresponds to the suggested shape on the card. It is the responsibility of the partner to spell the word that was read. If they are incorrect they the partner gives them a second chance before reading the correct spelling. If they are correct, or after they have received the correct spelling, then the other partner reads the word corresponding to the original shape suggested by the teacher. Students exchange cards and resume moving around using the next loco-motor skill designated by the teacher. This continues for as many rounds as the teacher deems appropriate.

Equipment required: 3 X 5 cards with shapes, such as a square, a circle, a triangle, a diamond. Next to each shape should be a vocabulary word or a variation of the same word, i.e., tense, plural, possessive, etc. There should be enough cards so that students can switch cards with the teacher if they have had the same card twice.

Teacher's notes:

Skip & Spell

Focus: Students will incorporate the designated loco-motor skill with a review of spelling or vocabulary lists.

Summary: Students will utilize knowledge of correct spelling from individual vocabulary lists to move around the alphabet letter area spelling the individual words.

Success criteria: The students will study their vocabulary list and attempt to remember the spelling of the words after having looked at the word only briefly.

Activity diagram: The area of participation should facilitate enough room for all the letters to be scattered randomly around on the surface with sufficient space between them to allow for students skipping at moderate speeds.

Activity description: The teacher will tell the students to skip (other loco-motor skills can be incorporated at any time to keep the activity interesting) from card to card spelling the vocabulary word. The teacher will either call out the words to the class as a whole or the students will be given an individual list and asked to look at the word and then recall how to spell it as they skip around the area.

Equipment required: Series of alphabet cards that represent the letters commonly found on the vocabulary list and representative of their frequency on the list.

Teacher's notes:

Sounds Like

Focus: The phonetic similarity of words is used to make associations for the students.

Summary: Students will distinguish the sounds of words that are similar and incorporate a loco-motor skill to complete a task set by the teacher.

Success criteria: The students will be familiar with the sounds of numbers and various words which when pronounced have similar phonetic sounds. These should be introduced and practiced in class initially and this becomes a supplementary activity.

Activity diagram: The space required will depend upon the number of students in the class. Students need only to stand up and move freely around the designated area. Enough room between seated students to enable the moving students to freely run, skip, gallop, or perform whatever the chosen loco-motor activity.

Activity description: The students will sit pretzel style on the floor. The students will be assigned a number that they are to remember and utilize throughout the course of the activity. The teacher will call out a word that has a similar phonetic sound to the number that they were assigned. When they can distinguish their number they are to stand up and move around the area using the prescribed loco-motor skill before returning to their original location on the floor and await the next word called by the teacher.

Equipment required: The teacher will need a list of numbers and corresponding words with similar phonetic sounds. This need not be limited to lower numbers any series can be used if the teacher devises the list of phonetic words. For example: nine-> fine, dine, spine, etc. In this case the teacher would still use a group of four students only their assigned number could be seven, eight, nine and ten.

Teacher's notes:

Spell Check Tag

Focus: A tag game will be utilized as a vehicle for the review of spelling or vocabulary words.

Summary: Students will utilize their ability to recall the correct spelling of vocabulary words in a game of tag.

Success criteria: The use of the class vocabulary lists will require that the students remain up to date with their knowledge and ability to recall the correct spelling of the words.

Activities diagram: The area required will be determined by the size of the class and the suggested loco-motor skill incorporated into the activity. If students are allowed to run for this activity then it will require more space simply to avoid collision. If the teacher suggests restrictive loco-motor skills a smaller area will be adequate.

Activity description: The teacher will select three or four students to be "taggers" for the initial round of play. Each of these students will be given some form of visual designation to wear such as a pinnie. Two of the students will be designated as "taggers" and the remaining one or two students will be the spell checkers, who will have a pile of 3 X 5 cards with the vocabulary word on them and a different colored pinnie. The "taggers" will attempt to move around the playing area using the suggested loco-motor skill and tag other players. When a player is tagged they must stop and remain in that spot until one of spell checkers (who will be given a different loco-motor skill to utilize) come to them. When a spell checker arrives at their spot they will use the 3 X 5 card from the top of the pile and request that the player correctly spell the word before returning to the game. If they are incorrect in their attempt at spelling the word then they must wait in that spot until another spell checker comes back to them. (On an incorrect attempt the spell checker should give the player the correct spelling before they move to the next tagged player.) The spell checker must move to another player before they go back to a player who has missed the correct spelling of a word. When they return to that player they will again use whatever word is on top of the pile.

Equipment required: A sufficient number of 3 X 5 cards with vocabulary words. These cards may also have the words used in sentences on the reverse side for the benefit of the students or to be used by the teacher as a flash card. Two different forms of visual designation for the "taggers" and the spell checkers.

Teacher's notes:

Spelling Unscramble

Focus: Color-coded letters from the class spelling or vocabulary lists will be distributed to the students for a review activity.

Summary: Students will utilize knowledge of the correct spelling of words from a vocabulary list in a loco-motor activity.

Success criteria: The students must be familiar with their current vocabulary list and must be capable of cooperating to form words in small groups.

Activity diagram: The area required will be large enough to permit the students to move freely using loco-motor skills without collision.

Activity description: Students will each receive a color-coded letter from a word on their current vocabulary list. They will be asked to use a specific loco-motor skill to move around the area while searching out other students who have letters of a similar color so they can form a word. When they have formed the word they will return to a central location using the loco-motor skill where they will randomly be given another letter and then return to the activity area to form another word. Students who do not find the members of their word should continue to perform the loco-motor skill around the area until students begin to return to the teacher for new letters.

Equipment required: The letters for each word on the vocabulary list should be color-coded or distinguishable in some fashion. There should be sufficient letter for all students and then additional letter which the teacher can distribute as the words are formed.

Teacher's notes:

Spelling Word Swing

Focus: Variations of root words will provide a challenge to students either in the form of spelling or using them in sentences.

Summary: The students will utilize various forms of a root word in spelling and vocabulary activities while cooperating with partners.

Success criteria: The students must be prepared to spell, use words in a sentence correctly, or perform some other type of activity decided by the teacher with the words on the cards that they will possess.

Activity diagram: Students will require enough space to freely move around the area using loco-motor skills selected by the teacher without fear of collision.

Activity description: Each student will be given a card with the four symbols and the four corresponding versions of the same root word. Such as, a red circle with the word "empty" printed in red; a blue square with the word "empties" printed in blue; a purple triangle with the word "emptied" printed in purple; and a green rectangle with the word "emptying" printed in green. The colors and shapes on each card may be different to allow the teacher to challenge the students; such as having the students spell the red word or use the circle word in a sentence, etc. The shapes may also signify some other portion of the curriculum such as planets or sign language symbols either of which would also be color-coded. Music can be used to set the tempo for the performing of a loco-motor skill while the students move around the playing area. When the music stops or on the signal given by the teacher the students will find a partner and face one another. The teacher will call out a shape or a color that will signify the version of the word that the students will use for their activity. The teacher will designate the activity the students are to perform. The activities may be spelling that version of the word, putting it into a sentence, identifying the correct form of the word, etc. The pairs of students will take turns using each other words from their card. If the designated task is done incorrectly the student may have another opportunity or as many opportunities as necessary to complete the task correctly in the time allotted or if there is question concerning the response they may approach the teacher for clarification. The teacher will signal the students to exchange cards and repeat the activity finding another partner on the teachers' next command. The teacher can change the loco-motor skill and the designated activity at any time.

Equipment required: Sufficient number of cards to allow the teacher to exchange cards with the students during the activity. A CD or tape player may be used to add background music.

Teacher's notes:

Story Lines

Focus: A review of previously read stories or materials from books is accomplished by using a small group activity.

Summary: Students will utilize their ability to recall information from a story or book read in class to construct sentences that relate to the story.

Success criteria: Students must recall the important elements of the story read in class and be able to construct sentences from key words.

Activity diagram: The area required must be large enough for the students to move around without fear of collision while they exchange cards with other students.

Activity description: The teacher will distribute laminated cards that will contain key words from a story or book read in class. The teacher will also assign the students to groups that will work together to collect cards for the sentence construction. Students will be assigned a loco-motor skill to perform as they move randomly around the room exchanging cards. When the teacher gives a designated signal they will get together with their group and use their cards (each card may be used only once each round) to make sentence that describe something which occurred in the story. These sentences will be written down on sheets of paper to share with the class later in the activity. After a period of time the students' return to use another loco-motor skill and exchange cards until the teacher determines the round is over and they may construct more sentences. This continues until the teacher wishes to have the groups share their sentences and discuss the story further.

Equipment required: Laminated cards with key words from the story or book read in class. Paper and writing instruments should be made available.

Teacher's notes:

Story Writers Tag

Focus: Random words written on clothespins become the focus for a creative writing activity.

Summary: The students will participate in a clothespin tag activity and utilize the acquired clothespins as the basis for a creative writing assignment.

Success criteria: The students must be capable of constructing sentences and paragraphs and be familiar with the concept of creative writing.

Activity diagram: The space required must allow for unobstructed participation in an activity where the students will chase and flee without fear of collision.

Activity description: Each student will receive three or four clothespins that they will cooperatively pin to each other's back in the area of their shoulder blades. The students will form teams of three or four and may not take any clothespins from their teammates. The teacher will designate a loco-motor skill to be used during the activity and give a signal to begin. Students will attempt to capture as many clothespins from other students as possible. When they have three additional clothespins they will move to a designated safe zone and attach them to their back as high as possible and return to the activity and capture more. After a given period of time the teacher will stop the activity and have the students return to their group, take the remaining clothespins off their backs and write down all the words on a sheet of paper. These words become the focus for a creative writing assignment to be conducted in class. The teacher can determine the appropriate use of any or all the captured words in the writing assignment.

Equipment required: Enough clothespins for each member of the class to have three or four.

Teacher's notes:

Toss n' Spell

Focus: Review activity for spelling or vocabulary lists using a tossing activity.

Summary: Students will demonstrate tossing skills in conjunction with correctly spelling vocabulary words in an attempt to complete a list of words.

Activity diagram: The area required would only need to be large enough to accommodate the tosses of the students from a desired distance onto the poster board laying flat on the floor.

Activity description: Pairs of students would work at each station. One student would begin by tossing a beanbag or some other object that does not roll onto the poster board. When the beanbag stops and comes to rest on a number their partner would look at the list to see what word corresponds to that number and ask for the correct spelling of that word. If the individual correctly spells the word they get another attempt. If the beanbag lands on the same number then they switch roles, if it lands on a new number they spell the new word. If the spelling attempt is incorrect their partner gives them a second chance before spelling it correctly from the list, then they would switch roles. Each player should attempt to toss to all the numbers on the board and spell all the words correctly in the time allotted for them at that learning station. The teacher can have more than one pair of vocabulary word lists at the station for the faster and more advanced students.

Equipment required: Poster board with circled numbers, pairs of vocabulary lists of varied difficulty and beanbags for tossing.

Teacher's notes:

Vocabulary Virus

Focus: Using a tag game format students will review vocabulary/spelling words.

Summary: Students will use their knowledge of the correct spelling of the class vocabulary words in a tag game format.

Success criteria: Students must be familiar with the correct spelling of any and all vocabulary words used in the class.

Activity diagram: The playing area will need to be large enough to accommodate the random movement associated with a chase and flee type activity, the designated loco-motor skill and the number of students participating.

Activity description: The teacher will designate a specific loco-motor skill to be utilized in this chase and flee activity. The teacher will randomly select a group of students to be the "chasers" initially and give them each a series of five cards and each one should have a colored pinnie to wear. The teacher will also designate a group of students to be the "healers." These students should be given a different colored pinnie to wear. The remainder of the class will be "fleers" who will attempt to move around the playing area without being tagged by the "chasers." If a "chaser" tags them then they are given a card with a vocabulary word printed on it. They will memorize the correct spelling of the word and then raise their hand high in the air. When a "healer" sees a raised hand they go over and take the card. The student who was tagged must spell the word correctly before they can return to the game. The "healer" can assist the tagged player in correctly spelling the vocabulary word when necessary. When a "healer" has collected five cards they return the vocabulary cards and the pinnie to the teacher and become a "fleer". After a "chaser" has tagged five students they return their pinnie to the teacher and become a "fleer". The teacher must periodically choose new groups of students to be "chasers" and "healers" to keep the game going. The teacher should have a sufficient number of vocabulary cards to rotate in new words throughout the activity.

Equipment required: Enough vocabulary cards to keep the students moving throughout the activity. Two sets of colored pinnies for the chasers and healers.

Teachers' notes:

Vowel Search

Focus: Loco-motor skills and random movement will be utilized as students locate similar vowels and words.

Summary: Students will use their knowledge of the vowels and vocabulary words to correctly group themselves.

Success criteria: The students will be aware of the difference between vowels and consonants. They will be familiar with a series of vocabulary words that they can spell from memory.

Activity diagram: The area required would be dependent upon the size of the class and the loco-motor skill utilized.

Activity description: The teacher will give each student a card with a vocabulary word on it. Each word will have one vowel that is printed in a different color to distinguish it from the other letters. The students will then utilize the suggested loco-motor skill to move around the area and locate other students who have a card with the same or different vowel highlighted, as determined by the teacher. When the students find another student or a group of students with a similar or different vowel they will link at the elbows and utilize the assigned loco-motor skill to continue until the have formed a group of however many the teacher determines appropriate. When the group size has been achieved they will all return to a central location and choose a new card. Their card should be placed face down on the floor and then they pick up another card and return to perform the suggested loco-motor skill and find a new group. This continues until the teacher changes the loco-motor skill or ends the activity.

Equipment required: A series of vocabulary cards with the vowels highlighted. There should be at least two cards for every student in the activity. Words can be repeated with different vowels highlighted.

Teachers' notes:

What Did You Spell?

Focus: A review of vocabulary or spelling words will be completed by having students form the letters of the words using their bodies as directed by the teacher.

Summary: Students will use their bodies to represent the shapes of letters for their partners to spell a word.

Success criteria: How to use the body to create letters and to give clues without talking can be practiced prior to engaging in this activity.

Activity diagram: The students will work in pairs or small groups and they will need enough room in order to prevent being distracted by another group. This could be accomplished in the classroom or in a large open area.

Activity description: Students will work in pairs or small groups and they will take turns acting out the letters of vocabulary words. Each student will take a new card and not show it to anyone else and attempt to make the letters with their bodies and have their partners guess the word they are spelling.

Equipment required: Each group should have a series of cards which contain all the vocabulary words the class is responsible for learning.

Teachers' notes:

Who Am I?

Focus: Students will use a chase and flee cooperative activity to review words groups.

Summary: Students will utilize a vocabulary list of words and definitions to participate in a match up game in a tag format.

Success criteria: Students will need to feel comfortable with individual words and also the meaning or definition of words.

Activity diagram: Students need an area adequate to utilize the suggested loco-motor skill free of obstacles and dangerous obstructions around the perimeter.

Activity description: Teacher will designate a group of students who will be the chasers and these students should be given a pinnie or some other type of clothing to indicate that they are a chaser. They will also be given a series of cards with vocabulary words on them. The remainder of the class should be given an individual card with a definition on it from the vocabulary list. The chasers must tag one of the fleers; at that time the fleer will read the definition to the chaser. The two students will look through the series of cards, which the chaser has to see if there is a match, this is a cooperative effort. If one of the chasers cards matches then the student who was the fleer and had the definition card will take both cards to the teacher who will give them a new definition card and they return to the game. The chaser immediately begins to chase another student. When the chaser is down to their last card, and can tag the student who has the correct definition, they take both cards to the teacher and give the pinnie or other designation to that student. Both students go to the teacher for new cards and return to the game. The duration of the activity is dependent upon the teacher and the interest of the students. [Remember the best time to end any activity is when the students are having the most fun, and then they will want to return to play at a later date.]

Equipment required: The teacher will need enough cards for the students to have vocabulary cards and definition cards. It will be a good idea to have duplicate and triplicate cards so that there is adequate opportunity to find matches.

Teachers' notes:

Wild Card Tag

Focus: A tag game format will be used to review vocabulary/spelling words.

Summary: Students will use vocabulary, eye-hand coordination and agility in a situation where they will collect letters to create words.

Success criteria: Students will use knowledge of spelling to create vocabulary words.

Activity diagram: The space required must be large enough to accommodate chase and flee type activity without fear of collision. An open grassy area would be best suited for the activity.

Activity description: Students will each receive a flag belt or two scarves to be tucked into their waistbands. They will also receive one card with a letter of the alphabet or a wild card on it. The players will randomly be placed in pairs or on a team. When the teacher has distributed the material the students will spread out around the area to begin the chase and flee activity. Each student will attempt to grab the scarves of any other student. If they successfully grab a scarf and have it in their hand they then get to keep that players letter. If that player has more than one letter then they get to randomly pick a card from the pile that the player will fan out in front of them. Once a player has lost their last letter they return to the home base (anywhere the teacher is standing) to receive a new letter prior to returning to the game. After a period of time, decided by the teacher, the students will get together with their partners or teammates and use their letter(s) to attempt to construct as many words as possible. They may use letter in a Scrabble type arrangement of up and down when possible. Again after a period of time they return to the game only this time they leave the letters they are able to use in words on the side and return with only the unused letter to play again. If they have used all their letters they simply go to the teacher for another to begin the activity. This process continues until the teacher decides the game is over.

Equipment required: Flag belts or scarves (cloth strips) and letter cards. There should be an abundant number of wild cards in the letter cards to be utilized by the students for spelling their vocabulary words. It would be suggested that the teacher have between five or six cards per player in the game for the first time to see how the student do in capturing letters.

Teachers' notes:

Word Scramble

Focus: Students use individual letters to form words from spelling/vocabulary lists.

Summary: Students will use word recognition skills to form words from random letters collected in a scramble format.

Success criteria: The recall of the correct spelling of the words on the vocabulary list will assist the students in quickly forming the words when all the letters are recovered.

Activity diagram: Students will be positioned behind a line or in an area. Hula-hoops, or some type of easily distinguishable area, should be placed 20 to 30 feet away. Inside the hula-hoops the letters of individual words should be placed face down in a random fashion.

Activity description: On the teachers command students will use the prescribed loco-motor skill to retrieve one letter at a time form the hoops, alternating hoops for retrieval. When all the letters have been retrieved the students will work to arrange the letters to form vocabulary words. They then write the word down on their list and return all the letters to their hoop face down. The teacher can change the loco-motor skill and scramble the letters within the hoops and begin again. The teacher can rotate the students around the stations so that they cannot read the words from the group on either side of them.

Equipment required: Enough letters and words for each pair of students to be at a separate station. Enough hula-hoops or some other object to form enough stations for each pair in the class. Students will carry pads of paper and pencils from station to station when writing down their words.

Teachers' notes:

Life Skills

Add 'em Up

Focus: The use of coins and calculating totals will be a group activity.

Summary: Student will utilize their ability to combine individual coins to calculate totals.

Success criteria: The students will have had experience with the calculation of totals from a variety of coins and are capable of doing these calculations either in their heads or on paper.

Activity diagram: Any area in which students can freely move about using a designated loco-motor skill.

Activity description: Students will be divided into groups and be sent to specific locations around the room. When the teacher gives the signal all the students will use the designated loco-motor skill to go to one of the containers in the center and take one coin. They will then return to their group location and wait until all members have returned and they will cooperatively add up the coins and record the total on the paper. Once they have completed that round they all go to another container and return to add the next total. The teacher must decide how may rounds the class will make and then the groups add their individual totals and they re-add all the coins to see if the totals match. The coins can be returned to their containers and the activity repeated with new groups or a new loco-motor skill or both.

Equipment required: Representations of coins in a variety of denominations, buckets or containers, sheets for recording totals.

Teacher's notes:

Bodies of Time

Focus: Telling time from the face of a clock or reading the numbers that represent specific time will be used in pairs.

Summary: Students will utilize their arms to represent the hands on a clock to practice their clock reading skills.

Success criteria: The students will need to be familiar with a traditional clock face and the distinction between the hour and minute hands on the clock. They will also need to know how to phrase the time represented by the hands of the clock.

Activity diagram: Students will require very limited space while working with partners the only consideration may be the noise distraction of pairs standing too close together while working out the problems.

Activity description: Students will establish a partner and the teacher will give the pair a series of cards. Each of the cards will have a clock face on one side with a specific time of the day designated by the hands and on the other side will be the time written out in number format. The partners will face the same direction with one in front of the other standing about five to six feet apart. The front student will look at the first card and depending on their level of knowledge with the clock can use either the clock side of the card or the number side. They will use one arm with a closed hand or fist as the hour indicator and a flat hand with fingers extended away from the arm as the minute indicator. If the hour is from six to twelve then the left arm is for hours and the right arm would indicate minutes and from one o'clock to five would be the opposite. After each partner has had a couple of turns they may get a new pile of cards and switch partners at the teachers discretion.

Equipment required: The teacher will need to make up a sufficient number of cards to provide each pair with a group of at least four so that each partner has two opportunities at each role.

Teacher's notes:

Destination Estimation

Focus: The concept of estimation for distances will be utilized in conjunction with varied loco-motor skills.

Summary: Students will develop and utilize a working knowledge of distances in various units.

Success criteria: The students will determine the average length of their walking stride and utilize this stride to estimate distances traveled and then how to convert to the requested unit of measurement.

Activity diagram: Any area where the teacher can pre-measure specific distances or courses for the students to walk will be appropriate.

Activity description: The teacher will construct a series of cards that list pathways or courses that the students will be responsible for traveling to determine the distances. Students will be requested to convert the distances into various units of measurement.

Equipment required: Pathway markers or courses marked for the students to travel. A series of cards with specific notations for the order in which the students are to travel and the units of measurement which they are requested to convert from their walking distances.

Teachers' notes:

Give 'n Take

Focus: Supply and demand concepts will be depicted in a tug-of-war activity.

Summary: Students will experience the effect of unequal distribution of players in a tug-o-war activity to simulate the concept of supply and demand.

Success criteria: The students must have a working knowledge of the concept of supply and demand and be capable of working in a goal oriented cooperative team effort.

Activity diagram: The teacher must determine the configuration of the class activity and select an area large enough to accommodate the number of tug-o-wars going on at the same time.

Activity description: The teachers should divide the class into sub-groups of two and three or four and five, depending on the number of students in the class. The groups of even numbers will conduct a tug-o-war against each other initially to see how comparable groups perform in this type of activity. Then the teacher will put groups that are uneven in number against each other, i.e. three against two or five against four to see the outcome of the same activity. The teacher will identify one group as "supply" and the other group as "demand" to demonstrate the point of how uneven supply and demand affects the outcome of the economics tug-o-war in the marketplace.

Equipment required: Enough tug-o-war ropes for the number of activities going on at the same time. Sufficient flags to signify the center in the rope and cones or markers to signify the boundaries for pulling the rope in a specific direction to win the round.

Teacher's notes:

Human Clock

Focus: Telling time and an awareness of the hands on a clock will be practiced by the students using their bodies in the activity.

Summary: The students will participate in an activity that will require cooperation among small groups to complete the tasks set forth by the teacher.

Success criteria: Students will be familiar with the face of a clock and the corresponding numbers and what they represent relative to twelve and twenty-four hours of the day. Students must also be aware of the need for cooperation in an activity that utilizes small groups.

Activity diagram: The teacher will determine what size groups are appropriate for the class and utilize as many clock areas as possible to provide adequate movement for all students. Each clock area will involve a circle large enough for the students to hold hands or link elbows and move in a circular pattern similar to the hands on a clock.

Activity description: Groups of students will be assigned to a clock area and then broken up into two uneven number groups (4 and 6; 3 and 4, 2 and 3, etc.). This will allow one group to represent the minute hand and the other to represent the hour hand on the clock. The students will hold hands or lock elbows and move in unison. One end of the line of students will act as though they are attached to the center of the clock face and move around that point. When the teacher calls out a specific time of the day and loco-motor skill the students must move to that corresponding location without letting go of the hands of the other members of their individual group. This means that they cannot pass the other group in their clock and must cooperate between the two groups. The teacher can call out a number of individual times and then devise a method to switch the students from minute hands to hour hands on their individual clock face or change to a new clock face.

Equipment required: Sets of cards with numbers corresponding to the face of a clock.

Teachers' notes:

Recycle Rally

Focus: Recycling materials and group decisions will assist in separating a variety of recycled material cards.

Summary: Students will take a proactive approach to the disposal of trash and recycling objects in a small team relay format.

Success criteria: The students will recall information from discussions concerning the disposal of materials in the trash and how many items can be easily recycled if properly identified.

Activity diagram: Any area in which students can freely move about using a designated loco-motor skill.

Activity description: The teacher will divide the class into small groups of three, four or five students each. The teacher will distribute a group of cards to each line of students and they will place them face down at the beginning of their line. The smaller the group the better so that each student gets numerous chances to make decisions on the pictures that are on the card selected. Each group will line up one behind the other facing the same direction. The first student will select a card from the pile in front of their group. They will pass the card between their legs to the next student in line they will take the card and pass it over their head to the student behind them who, in turn, passes it between their legs, etc. This continues until the last student in the line takes the card and uses the designated loco-motor skill to go to the area of the room designated for trash disposal/recycling area. Containers will be labeled according to their type of recycling use or as trash for item designated as not being recyclable. That student then returns to their line and becomes the first person in line and selects a card to start passing the card to the back of the line. This continues until all the cards have been placed in containers. The teacher then brings the students together and the containers together to go through the containers and see if all the cards have been placed in the proper containers. This discussion will reinforce the concepts covered in the classroom setting concerning the environmental impact of trash disposal and recycling.

Equipment required: Numerous cards with pictures of foods and food containers to enable the students to handle them easily.

Teacher's notes:

Season's Greetings

Focus: Holiday specific vocabulary/spelling words are reviewed in a tag game format.

Summary: Students will engage in an activity that makes them consider those elements of their life that make them happy for who they are and what they have.

Success criteria: Students will need to be presented with the vocabulary list during class time and then practice spelling these words that are appropriate for them.

Activity diagram: The location of this activity is dependent upon how the teacher structures the game. If there were a blackboard available in a large enough area to allow running, skipping, galloping, etc. then this would be ideal. If there is no area with a blackboard and one cannot be brought in for the activity, then pieces of newsprint or poster board can be used for the students to write on.

Activity description: Designated students must chase the other students with the intention of tagging them. The students who are "taggers" must be given some type of distinguishing article of clothing to wear. Pinnies are the easiest articles of clothing to quickly change. When a student is tagged they take the pinnie from the "tagger" and move to the blackboard or poster board and write down a word or phrase that is part of their spelling or vocabulary list with a holiday theme. Then they return to the game and attempt to tag someone other than the person who tagged them. This continues as long as the teacher is satisfied with the activity. The words written on the blackboard then become the focus for a review as the teacher points them out to the class for discussion.

Equipment required: Blackboard, poster board, newsprint, etc. Writing instruments appropriate for the surface utilized.

Teachers' notes:

Time's Up

Focus: Students will review the face of a clock and telling time from the position of the hands on the clock.

Summary: The students will utilize the time of the day listed on their card to properly position themselves on the face of a clock in a large open area.

Success criteria: Students must understand the notation for the time of day and the corresponding relative positions on the face of a clock.

Activity diagram: The teacher must designate an area large enough for the students to be able to stand in a circle shoulder to shoulder without contacting one another. This should include markings for the hours and each fifteen-minute interval.

Activity description: The teacher will distribute enough cards for each student to have one. The teacher will designate a loco-motor skill and the students will move around the open area exchanging cards with other students at random. When the teacher gives a signal the students must find their appropriate spot on the face of the clock that is drawn or designated on the surface of the playing area. After they have all found their correct spot the teacher will designate a new loco-motor skill and the students will randomly exchange cards, wait for the teachers' signal and repeat the activity until the students have become familiar with all the appropriate locations on the face of the clock.

Equipment required: A series of laminated cards beginning with twelve fifteen and progressing at fifteen minute intervals until the series is finished with eleven forty-five including the hours such as one o'clock, two o'clock, etc. The series will be forty-eight cards in all.

Teacher's notes:

Tree Sense

Focus: A tag game format is used to promote a discussion concerning the disparity between development and environmental concerns.

Summary: Students will participate in a tag game format to experience the concept of development and deforestation.

Success criteria: Students will utilize their ability to participate in a tag game format.

Activity diagram: The students will need an area large enough to utilize the suggested loco-motor skills in an obstacle free environment.

Activity description: The total number of students should be divided into an odd number of groups; 3, 5 or 7. The teacher will then divide the groups in half, purposely having an uneven number in each group. One group will be given one color pinnie and the other a second color pinnie. Each student will get a flag belt and two flags. The teacher will designate a loco-motor skill that can be used by the students. When the teacher gives the signal to begin the students attempt to steal flags from members of the other team. When a student has captured two flags they go to the teacher who will give them a tree cutout to put into their teams' bag. If a student has lost both of their flags s/he must go to the safe zone and put on two more to return to the game. After the student have played for a specific amount of time the teacher will stop the game and the students will count the number of trees which are in their team's bag. The teacher will lead a discussion about the number of trees each team has and talk about how one team might be developers and each tree represents one which they are cutting down in the name of development and the other team are environmentalists and each tree represents one which they either save from the developers or one which they plant. The uneven team configuration is used to demonstrate the disparity in the world between developers and environmentalists.

Equipment required: Spring loaded clothespins, tree cutouts, pinnies.

Teacher's notes:

Which Way Do We Go?

Focus: Utilization of directional awareness and reading skills are reinforced.

Summary: Students will utilize their knowledge surrounding the concept of direction to respond to tasks set by the teacher.

Success criteria: The general sense of direction should be complimented by classroom practice with points of the compass. The use of loco-motor skills that they are familiar with will make the activity more enjoyable.

Activity diagram: A large open area is necessary. There should be adequate space for the students to move and change direction without fear of collision.

Activity description: The students will get into small groups (the teacher must ensure that at least one member of the group can read the cards). Each group will be assigned to a sign: north, south, east or west. The group will take a card from the pile and follow the directions listed on the card. When they have used all the cards at their sign they will move to the next sign in a clockwise fashion until they have been to all the directional locations. This activity can lead to map reading and directional puzzles.

Equipment required: Directional instruction cards for the locations and groups. Location signs for north, south, east and west

Teachers' notes:

Mathematics

Balloon Math

Focus: Basic mathematic skills are utilized in conjunction with tapping and catching a balloon.

Summary: Students will utilize their ability to add, subtract and multiply while using eye-hand coordination to tap and catch a balloon spinning in the air.

Success criteria: Knowledge of addition, subtraction and multiplication dependent upon the requirements of the curriculum for the students developmentally appropriate level.

Activity diagram: The area needed for this activity is limited to that required for partners to stand and toss or tap a balloon back and forth. The aisle in between desks may be sufficient. The teacher may decide to expand the activity to allow the students to keep the balloons in the air while walking or skipping until they hear a signal and then they catch the balloon with both hands. This would require a larger unobstructed area for safety.

Activity description: Students will work either in partners or alone to keep a balloon in the air. When the teacher gives a signal one or the other will start with the balloon. The teacher will call out an operation to be performed with the two numbers: addition, subtraction or multiplication. If the students are working alone then they perform the designated operation with whatever numbers are given. If they are working with a partner then they both call out the answer and they begin to tap the balloon back and forth the correct number of times for the correct answer. This continues with the partners alternating roles beginning the tapping.

Equipment required: Either one balloon per child in class or one balloon per pair.

Teachers' notes:

Bizz Buzz

Focus: Recognition of the multiplications tables is utilized in a cooperative race format.

Summary: The students will utilize their ability to count in various multiples of numbers and remain aware of various responsibilities within a game format.

Success criteria: Students must be able to participate in a loco-motor skill and at the same time count and know the multiples of numbers determined by the teacher.

Activity diagram: The students will need an area large enough to allow the group to hold hands and utilize a loco-motor skill in a circular formation. Students must also be able to move around the outside of the circle in an attempt to return to their original position.

Activity description: Students will form a large circle and hold hands. The teacher will pick a loco-motor skill for the students to perform while they move around. The teacher will then select a number (or numbers for an advanced group) for the students to concentrate on while counting around the circle. Each student will count the subsequent number. Each time a student counts a number that is a multiple of the original number they must say either Bizz or Buzz and then the next student continues the counting. If a student neglects to say the proper number or forgets to say Bizz or Buzz at the appropriate time they must circle the entire group using the same loco-motor skill before the counting returns to their spot. If the class can accurately get to their spot counting around the circle before they return then they must continue to move around the outside of the circle.

Equipment required: None

Teachers' notes:

Blow Up

Focus: Mathematics calculations determining the number of repetitions for exercises or activities.

Summary: Students will utilize mathematics and listening skills to perform the correct number of repetitions for activities according to the results of individual problems.

Success criteria: The student must be capable of performing mathematics calculations found on a piece of paper on the inside of the balloon and perform all the suggested activities or exercises.

Activity diagram: Area large enough for the class to participate in the suggested activities safely.

Activity description: The teacher must design small slips of paper that can be inserted into balloons before they are blown up. The teacher will randomly select students to choose an inflated balloon and find a method of breaking the balloon. Once the balloon is broken the student will read the activity description and then read the math problem. Each student will think of the solution in their head and perform the correct number of repetitions individually. A second student is then chosen to break the next balloon and this continues until all the balloons are broken.

Equipment required: Enough balloons and slips of paper for the entire class.

Teachers' notes:

Dog Gone

Focus: Mathematic equations will be employed as students are required to find partners as they move around the area performing a loco-motor skill.

Summary: Students will utilize basic concepts of addition and subtraction or multiplication and division to answer problems assigned by the teacher using Dalmatian Math Cards.

Success criteria: Students need to grasp the basic concepts of addition and subtraction at the lower levels and multiplication or division at the upper levels to complete the problems assigned by the teacher.

Activity diagram: Since this will be a cooperative activity the movement area can be limited to that needed for freedom of movement utilizing designated loco-motor skills.

Activity description: Each student will be given one card or a series of cards depending on the method that the teacher wishes to take for the activity. On each card there will be a drawing of a Dalmatian puppy with a specific number of spots on it. That number of spots is the number that they may use for that particular card to solve the problem designated by the teacher. The teacher will designate the loco-motor skill to be used by the class as they move around the area randomly. The teacher will then call out either a mathematics equation or the solution to a mathematics sentence and the students must move around the area to locate other students with whom the will match up to address the solution to the problem posed by the teacher.

Equipment required: Cards with the drawing of Dalmatian puppies on them with a specific number of spots on each card. The teacher must produce a list of equations or mathematics problems or sentences that the students must address.

Teacher's notes:

Flash Card Frenzy

Focus: Toss and catch skills between partners are used with mathematics flash cards.

Summary: Students will utilize ball skills to perform designated tasks of tossing or bouncing to complete the flash card problems.

Success criteria: Students will use this as a review activity for addition and subtraction problems.

Activity diagram: The size of the area should allow students to choose the distance between each other so they can toss and catch a ball.

Activity description: Each pair of students will receive a stack of flash cards with mathematic sentences on them. The pair will begin with the top card that has an incomplete mathematic sentence designated and toss or bounce a ball between them the number of times designated by the correct answer for the flash card equation. Once they have completed the number of tosses or bounces they turn the card over to see if they were correct. They then do the same for the next card in the pile until they have completed the entire pile. When the finish each card in the pile they go to the teacher and get a new stack and continue the process.

Equipment required: Either commercially produced flash cards or home made flash cards but enough for each group to have a pile with extras that the teacher can distribute when the students finish their individual pile.

Teacher's notes:

Freeze Tag

Focus: Freeze tag format is utilized to review basic mathematic sentences.

Summary: The students will demonstrate their mathematics skills of addition and subtraction in a freeze tag game where the solution or the problem can be used to return to play.

Success criteria: The students will rely on their ability to think of as many solutions to mathematics problems as possible.

Activity diagram: Students will require enough space to freely move in a chase and flee type activity without fear of collision.

Activity description: The teacher will distribute flash cards that will have addition and subtraction problems on one side and the correct answers on the other. A group of students will be designated as "taggers" and carry some type of colored article which is easily visible. They will attempt to tag the remainder of the class. When a student is tagged they must stand still, with their feet spread apart, holding either the problem side or the solution side facing away from them. They will remain in the frozen position until another student who has the correct opposite of their card [problem or solution] comes to unfreeze them by passing their card under the frozen players' legs. Students who are not frozen may use either side of their flash cards while they are moving around to unfreeze the other players. Once a player has been unfrozen they must go to the teacher and exchange their card for another one before returning to the game. After the "tagger" has frozen six players they come to the teacher to turn in their colored article and return to the game as an unfrozen player. The teacher will arbitrarily give the colored article to another player to be "tagger" until they tag six players and so on.

Equipment required: A series of flash cards that have similar solutions and problems that are interchangeable for all the students' mathematics ability levels.

Teachers' notes:

Guess What!?!

Focus: Distance estimation and an awareness of their loco-motor skills are the focus in this activity.

Summary: Students will participate in an activity that requires an estimation of the number of repetitions of individual loco-motor skills necessary to travel a specific distance.

Success criteria: The student must be familiar with the individual loco-motor skills and have the ability to utilize them in a linear fashion to cover distance.

Activity diagram: The space required will be dependent upon the students' ability to use this estimate quality and perform variations of individual loco-motor skills. The area should be at least the size of an average gymnasium.

Activity description: The class will either work individually or in small groups to complete a course which is comprised of a series of distances, each one of which requires the students to utilize a different loco-motor skill determined by the teacher in advance. The students will initially estimate how many of the individual loco-motor movements (i.e., hops, skips, slides, etc.) will be required to move across the prescribed distance and record their estimate on the sheet provided. They will then proceed to attempt to cover the distance and count the actual number and record that number in the appropriate space. This can be repeated at different distances as many times as the teacher feels it is beneficial using any number of loco-motor skills.

Equipment required: Individual or group estimate charts, pencils for recording estimates and markers for the course.

Teachers' notes:

The Human Solution

Focus: A cooperative approach will be utilized to reinforce basic math skills.

Summary: Students will cooperate to form groups that represent the solution to mathematics problems posed by the teacher as they utilize assigned loco-motor skills.

Success criteria: The students need to be capable of mentally solving problems and performing the assigned loco-motor skills.

Activity diagram: Any large open space for the utilization of the assigned loco-motor skill will be sufficient.

Activity description: The class will be assigned a specific loco-motor skill to perform individually in a random formation. The teacher will call out a basic mathematics problem for which the solution is a number less than half the total number of students in the class. The students will call out the solution and while performing the loco-motor skill they will form groups that represent the number in the solution. They will hold hands and continue to perform the loco-motor skill until the teacher requests that they separate before giving the next problem and assigning a new loco-motor skill. This will continue as long as the students are capable of successfully participating.

Equipment required: The teacher will have a list of appropriate problems and loco-motor skills.

Teachers' notes:

Leapfrog

Focus: Basic addition and subtraction activities are utilized in conjunction with leapfrog.

Summary: Students will work cooperatively to complete the solution to a mathematics problem suggested by the teacher.

Student preparation: The students will need to be capable of cooperatively calculating the mathematics solution and participate in the leapfrog activity respecting each other's potential and limitations.

Activity diagram: The teacher can either line the students up on one side of a given area and ask the students to cross the area using the leap frog technique or the teacher can allow the students to use a random formation and self designed pathways to continue moving around the room using the leap frog technique. In either case a space that is free of obstruction will be required to provide the safest environment.

Activity description: The students will select a partner or work as a group of three, if necessary. The teacher will instruct them as to the manner in which they will move, either directly across the given area or in a random fashion. The teacher will then give them a mathematics problem for which they will devise a solution and make the appropriate number of jumps, counting each time one person leaps over the other.

Equipment required: A list of appropriate mathematics equations.

Teacher's notes:

Loco-motor Finger Throw

Focus: In pairs, small or large groups students will calculate mathematic sentences formed by "throwing fingers."

Summary: Students will utilize basic mathematics functions to solve problems set forth by the teacher in pairs or small groups while performing a prescribed loco-motor skill.

Success criteria: The students will utilize their present knowledge of mathematics to solve problems suggested by the teacher with a partner or in a small group after performing the prescribed loco-motor skill.

Activity diagram: The space required will be dependent upon the size of the class and the desired activity level of the participants. Generally a small gymnasium or multi-purpose area would be sufficient indoors.

Activity description: The teacher will ask the students to move around the designated activity area using a specified loco-motor skill. When the teacher calls out a number (twos, threes, fours, etc.) the students will form the appropriate size group, throw fingers* from one or two hands on the count of three and perform the mathematics function suggested by the teacher (addition, subtraction, multiplication or division). When a student has a suggested answer the remaining student(s) will verify or question the solution if a discrepancy exists the teacher may intervene when requested. Students will return to the prescribed loco-motor skill and form a new group when the teacher gives the next signal. This continues until the teacher changes the loco-motor skill or the activity. If the teacher senses a level of fatigue among the students they can adjust the loco-motor skill to allow for a recovery period.

*Throwing fingers refers to the activity where students count one, two, and on the number three they project one or two hands forward and allow a random number, from none (closed fist) to five, of fingers extended on each hand.

Equipment required: None

Teacher's notes:

Math Equation

Focus: Students will cooperate to create basic mathematic sentences from a series of cards distributed by the teacher.

Summary: Students will use their knowledge of addition, subtraction and multiplication to work cooperatively to devise problems.

Success criteria: Knowledge of the operations used in this activity and the ability to think critically to devise mathematics sentences that compute the suggested totals.

Activity diagram: The teacher can decide on the loco-motor skill or the type of movement they wish to incorporate during this activity and then decide upon the area suitable for the level of participation.

Activity description: Students will take two cards each. On both sides of each card there will be either numbers or designated operations symbols (there can be one of each on the same card). When the students are presented a card they must use the designated loco-motor skill and organize themselves so that in a group (no less than two students) their cards total the suggested number by adding, subtracting, multiplying or dividing combinations of the numbers found on the cards. There should be a series of extra cards that students may retrieve to satisfy the number if the cards that they are holding do not meet the requirements.

Equipment required: A series of cards with numbers and operation symbols listed randomly on both sides. A sufficient amount so that each student has two and there are plenty for substitute retrieval.

Teacher's notes:

Math Freeze

Focus: Basic mathematic operations are used as a vehicle for a freeze tag game.

Summary: Students will utilize their knowledge of the basic mathematics operations in a tag game while performing designated loco-motor skills.

Success criteria: The students will be required to perform basic mathematics operations without the use of pencil and paper.

Activity diagram: The teacher will decide the type of loco-motor skills to be utilized by the students and select an appropriate area for the students to move freely without collision.

Activity description: Each student will be given a set of cards (the number will be determined by the teacher). The teacher will select two or more students (depending upon the size of the class) to be "taggers" and give them some form of identification; pinnies, T-shirts, etc. The teacher will designate the loco-motor skill to be used by all the students. The students who are "taggers" will attempt to move around the playing area and tag individual students. When they are able to tag an individual student they will ask the student to solve a mathematics problems from one of their cards. If the students' answer is correct then they exchange one card each and the "taggers" continues to chase other students. The tagged student must now stand still and wait for another student to come up and they ask the same question to the new student. If the second student is correct in answering the question then both return to playing the game using the appropriate loco-motor skill. If the student is incorrect then they exchange cards and the only original student can return to play. When the original "tagger" tags a student and the answer that they give to the mathematics question is incorrect they become "tagger" and take the pinnie or T-shirt and the original "tagger" joins the other students.

Equipment required: A series of cards that will be the basis of the tag game. A sufficient number should be provided. Items to designate the individuals who are "tagger."

Teachers' notes:

Movement Solutions

Focus: The answer to basic mathematic sentences describes the number of repetitions for loco-motor movements utilized.

Summary: The students will move utilizing a prescribed loco-motor skill either individually or in small groups to the solution of a given mathematics problem.

Success criteria: The student will need to be comfortable with mathematics problems and possess sufficient listening skills to complete the tasks assigned by the teacher without pencil and paper.

Activity diagram: The area required must be large enough for either the individual movement of the class members or the small groups to move together using various loco-motor skills.

Activity description: The teacher will either place the class in small groups or ask the class to spread out randomly in the prescribed area. The teacher will then read a mathematics problem from their list (i.e., 5 + 4=) and provide a desired loco-motor skill (i.e., skipping, sliding, etc.) and the class will respond with the appropriate number of movements (9 skips or slides, etc.). This will continue with the students moving in random directions.

Equipment required: Lists of mathematics problems and loco-motor skills.

Teacher's notes:

Number Jumble

Focus: Loco-motor movements and basic mathematic calculations are utilized.

Summary: The students will utilize various mathematics operations in conjunction with loco-motor skills to demonstrate their ability to analyze problems cooperatively.

Success criteria: The students will perform the mathematical operations utilized in this activity mentally and they must be capable of working in pairs or small groups to solve the problems.

Activity diagram: Number stations will be randomly place around the playing area and the students will be given a loco-motor skill to perform while moving from one station to the next depending upon the result of the operation performed. The area will need to be large enough to allow for freedom of movement between stations by the pairs or small groups.

Activity description: Students will be organized in pairs or small groups to participate. Each group or pair will have a pencil and paper. The teacher will either assign a number to the group or have them select a number according to a random criterion (the total of the digits in their birthday, the total of the last number of their street address, etc.). The teacher will then give them some type of operation to perform with their number (such as; add four...). They will then utilize a loco-motor skill to move to the next station that represents the product of the operation. The teacher can also specify how many stations they must travel to in order to reach the correct total. Example would be to travel to four stations to reach the total for the number 23. They could go to stations 9, 7, 5 and 2. They would then record their travels. Each time they were given a problem they should write down both the problem and the method of solution on their paper.

Equipment required: Station number cards that represent all the possible combinations of numbers or operations to be performed by the students. A list of problems that the teacher intends to utilize to reinforce the operations performed in the classroom curriculum.

Teacher's notes:

Number Line

Focus: Small groups of students will work together to solve mathematical sentences.

Summary: Students will cooperate in small groups to complete mathematics problems posed by the teacher while utilizing specific loco-motor skills.

Success criteria: The students must have the listening skills to hear the problem and the concentration skills to solve it while they listen. They must then cooperate to correctly utilize the assigned loco-motor skill for the solution of the problem.

Activity diagram: Any large open area of sufficient size to accommodate the number of small groups within the class.

Activity description: The teacher will ask the students to form groups of three or four and stand shoulder to shoulder in a straight line. One end of the line will be addition or plus end and the other will be the subtraction or minus end. All of the groups should be in a random formation so as not to designate winners and losers and to take the focus off of what the other groups are doing. The teacher will read a problem, such as, 3 + 2= and the student at the addition or plus end will pass to the other end of the line using the prescribed loco-motor skill, this change from one end of the line to the other will signify "one" and when the second player moves down it will signify "two" and so on until five players have switched positions. If the problem were a subtraction problem then the student at the other end of the line would have started and the sequence should be reversed. As each student passes from one end to the other using the assigned loco-motor skill they should call out their number until the correct number is called.

Equipment required: The teacher should have a list of problems that are developmentally appropriate for the age group.

Teacher's notes:

Numbers Up!

Focus: Tossing and catching skills will be utilized as a result of mathematic sentence solutions.

Summary: The students will utilize their mathematics skill to respond to a problem and react to catching a tossed ball.

Success criteria: The students will react quickly to the problems set by the teacher and determine what is the appropriate action to be taken in response. The students must be prepared to analyze their number in relation to the problems set in the group activity.

Activity diagram: The number of students will determine the area and the number of groups used in the activity. Older children will need more room to be successful and enjoy the activity.

Activity description: The students will be broken up into groups of identical size. The number of students in the group should be kept below five to allow adequate opportunity to participate. Each student in the group will have a number and it may relate to the problems set forth by the teacher. The player in the group who has the ball will be asked to toss the ball at least ten feet high. Immediately after the teacher says toss s/he will give the problem for the students to decide who is responsible for catching the ball. When a student recognizes their number they are to step into the circle and catch the ball in the prescribed manner. This could be before it bounces, after it bounces once, etc. The task set should be developmentally appropriate to the age group and ability level. There need not be points awarded or winners and loser. The activity can simply be for the fun of listening and attempting to catch the ball. Students can be reassigned numbers and a new set of problems can be quickly utilized.

Equipment required: Enough balls for each group to have one. The teacher will need a series of numbers and computations to ensure that all students have equal opportunity to catch and toss the ball.

Teacher's notes:

Odds Are Best

Focus: The concept of odd and even numbers is used to calculate a mathematic sentence.

Summary: Students will utilize a prescribed mathematics operation to calculate a total that equals an odd number in conjunction with a partner.

Success criteria: The students must be capable of performing mathematics operations in their head and understand the difference between odd and even numbers.

Activity diagram: The area for the activity should be large enough for the students to move freely using the designated loco-motor skill without fear of collision.

Activity description: Each student will be given a laminated card with a number on it corresponding to the developmental level of the class. They will also be given a piece of paper and a pencil to record their mathematics sentences. The teacher will give a signal and the designated loco-motor skill that the students are to utilize as they move around the area. Initially the students are to exchange cards with everyone they meet until the teacher gives a second signal. The second signal initiates the time period in which the students are to find as many other individuals as possible whose numbers when used in a mathematics sentence with their own total an odd number. They are to write down the mathematics sentence before they continue on and attempt to find another student. After a given period of time the teacher will stop the activity to check the mathematics sentences. Then he students will exchange cards and begin again.

Equipment required: Laminated number cards that the students can pass back and forth. Provide enough pencils and pieces of paper for the entire class to use during the activity to write their answers.

Teacher's notes:

Parachute Numbers

Focus: The parachute will be the vehicle for review of concepts in mathematics.

Summary: Students will utilize basic mathematics skills and awareness of numbers to respond to questions posed by the teacher while working cooperatively with a parachute.

Success criteria: The knowledge of number combinations and simple operations with basic numbers will be essential. The use of advance thinking and computation skills may be developmentally appropriate in some situations.

Activity diagram: Sufficient room will be required depending upon the number and size of parachute utilized. The students should have enough room to safely run under the inflated parachute and out the opposite side without fear of collision with walls, other students or surrounding equipment.

Activity description: The students will be assigned a number and be told to find a spot around the outer edge of the parachute. On the teachers command the students will slowly raise the parachute above their heads and hold it up while it completely inflates. After the students have done this a few times to get accustom to the movement of the parachute the teacher will ask them to think about their number and then before they begin to raise the parachute the teacher will call out a specific number. When the parachute is completely inflated the students who have the suggested number will travel under the parachute using a controlled loco-motor skill without touching any other student and cross to the opposite side and re-grasp the edge of the parachute. After all the assigned numbers have had the opportunity to attempt the crossing the teacher will now change the task to using mathematics operations to determine the numbers which cross. An example would be: all those whose number equals five minus two cross now... this should be continued to allow all students to have a second opportunity to cross and then the operations can begin to get more difficult and include higher number or more difficult operations.

Equipment required: A sufficient number of parachutes to provide adequate opportunity for all students to raise and lower the parachute and to be able to cross under.

Teacher's notes:

Pocket Change

Focus: Coin denominations and monetary totals are used to review curricular materials.

Summary: Students must use the concept of denominations of money to calculate the amount of change required to total a specific amount call out by the teacher.

Success criteria: Students must be capable of calculating coinage totals and recognizing what the need for make up the difference between what they have and the suggested total.

Activity diagram: Any area in which students can freely move about using a designated loco-motor skill.

Activity description: The teacher will set up stations that represent the denominations of coins: pennies, nickels, dimes, quarters, and half-dollars. These stations should be randomly placed around the room. Each student will be given a set of coins at random in a cup or bag and be told to find a "home spot" in the area. The teacher will ask them to pick out one coin at random and hold it. The teacher will then tell the students what loco-motor skill they are to use during each round. The teacher will then call out a total; such as, sixty-three cents. The students must then take their first coin and look around the room and move to each of the stations from which they will need to secure coins to have a total of sixty-three cents when they return to their "home spot." After all the student have returned to their individual "home spots" the teacher will tell them to make a separate pile for each round of the activity. After the number of rounds that corresponds to the number of coins which the students started with, the teacher will give them the overall total that they should have. The students then count all the coins and see if they have the correct overall total in coins. The coins can then be returned to their individual containers and the activity started over as many times as the teacher determines to be appropriate.

Equipment required: Sufficient coin representations for the students to have ample opportunity to succeed in the activity.

Teacher's notes:

Puzzle Panic

Focus: A puzzle format in conjunction with mathematic sentences will determine the activity level of pairs of students.

Summary: Students will use loco-motor skills to collect puzzle pieces and perform an activity after solving a mathematics sentence.

Success criteria: The students must be capable of solving the mathematics problems on the construction paper and also need to be able to read or distinguish the activity descriptor on the back of the puzzle.

Activity diagram: The area should be large enough to provide students freedom of movement using prescribed loco-motor skills while moving in pairs.

Activity description: The class will be divided into pairs or small groups of three or four. The teacher will have distributed the pieces of the construction paper puzzles in different locations. The students will be instructed to hold hands or link elbows and to use a specific loco-motor skill to retrieve the pieces of the puzzle one at a time from each location and return to their home spot to drop it off and then retrieve another one. When they can assemble the pieces into a full sheet they will determine the solution to the mathematics sentence and use the solution to complete the activity descriptor on the reverse side of the puzzle. Activities can be exercises, nonsense movements (such as touch your elbow to your toe, touch your knee to the ground, etc.) or silly activities like singing Yankee Doodle. The solution to the math problem should be the focus. When they have finished the puzzle they must return the pieces to their locations and begin again retrieving a new colored puzzle. This continues until the class has been through all the puzzle colors or the teacher determines it is time to move on to another activity. Remember the best time to stop is when the class is having fun!

Equipment requirements: Enough puzzles to keep the class occupied with as many pairs or groups as deemed necessary. Markers of some sort for the locations of the individual puzzle pieces.

Teacher's notes:

Quick Solution Freeze Tag

Focus: Mental calculations are utilized to release players from the frozen position in the game.

Summary: Students will utilize their knowledge of mathematics to assist fellow students in a tag game.

Success criteria: The students must be capable of solving basic mathematics problems without the use of paper and pencil.

Activity diagram: The students can be limited to specific loco-motor skills or allowed to run if sufficient space is available. The size of the class and the size of the individual students will be factors to consider.

Activity description: A small group of students will be chosen to be "taggers". They will be given a pinnie to distinguish them from the other students. They will also receive a series of cards to distribute to those students they tag. The teacher will announce the loco-motor skill to be used in the game. The students who are "taggers" will prepare to chase the other students. When a student is tagged, the ""tagger"" will give them one of the cards. The tagged student will stand in that spot and hold up their card with the mathematics equation facing away and the answer facing toward them. As a student is moving past the stationary-tagged player, they attempt to solve the problem by shouting out the correct answer. When the correct answer is provided the player who was holding the card runs to the teacher to return that card. After a sufficient number of cards have been returned to the teacher a new group of students can be selected to be "taggers" and the activity can begin again.

Equipment required: Pinnies to distinguish the group of "taggers" players. Individual 5 X 8 equation cards to provide sufficient activity.

Teacher's notes:

Quick Thinking

Focus: A review of appropriate mathematic curricular material will be conducted using a toss and catch format.

Summary: Students will utilize their knowledge mathematics calculations while participating in toss and catch activities.

Success criteria: Students must be prepared to perform the requested calculations in their head while playing a game of catch.

Activity diagram: Students may choose the distance between each other and should not overlap another pair. The area will need to be large enough to accommodate all the pairs comfortably.

Activity description: Students will be allowed to pair up with an individual with similar skill and intellectual level to participate in this activity. The teacher will select developmentally appropriate mathematics curriculum: addition, subtraction, multiplication, etc. for the students to utilize. One student will have a ball and they will think of a calculation or mathematics sentence in their head before they toss the ball. The partner receiving the ball must call out the answer to the problem before catching the ball. The parameters should be developmentally appropriate also. The ball can bounce or be tossed high in the air or whatever the teacher determines to be appropriate. The students can challenge themselves to call out the correct answer before the ball touches the ground or bounces a second time or whatever is appropriate. Emphasis must be placed on controlled tosses to provide adequate opportunity for the partner to catch the ball.

Equipment required: Balls that provide an adequate bounce for the activity.

Teacher's notes:

Relievio

Focus: Mathematic sentences are utilized as a release mechanism in a tag game format.

Summary: The students will utilize their math skills to solve problems as a means to return to the game.

Success criteria: The students must be capable of solving simple mathematics problems in their heads.

Activity diagram: The area required can be restricted by the use of loco-motor skills to slow student movements. It need only be large enough to allow for random movement without collision while using the assigned loco-motor skill.

Activity description: The teacher will select a small group of students to be "taggers" initially. There will be a second group of initial "relievers" or "releasers" in the base area. The remainder of the class will be the group who is attempting to get away. The teacher will designate a loco-motor skill appropriate to the area and age group. When the signal is given to begin the students who are "taggers" will attempt to tag the other students. When a student is tagged they go to the home base area and one of the "relievers" picks out a math card from the bag and reads the problem to the student who was just tagged. If they can answer the problem correctly then they switch with the "reliever" and the "reliever" goes out into the game to be chased. If the problem is answered incorrectly the "reliever" tells them the answer and gets another card out of the bag. This continues until they can answer a card correctly and then they switch roles. The "relievers" are continually switching. Only the group that begins as "taggers" is constant. After a few minutes the teacher should rotate the group of students who are "taggers" so they don't get too tired. [This activity can be used for spelling or vocabulary by switching the information on the cards.]

Equipment required: 3 X 5 cards with math problems and solutions on them. Pinnies for the "taggers" group to wear.

Teacher's notes:

Shape Scramble

Focus: A review of geometric shapes and terms related to the shapes in a small group activity.

Summary: Students will cooperate in small groups to form shapes with pieces of rope from clues and terms provided by the teacher.

Success criteria: The students will utilize their knowledge of geometric shapes to produce rope representations of the perimeter for each of the shapes chosen.

Activity diagram: This would be best accomplished in a large open space to provide sufficient space for the groups of students to place their individual shapes on the ground or floor.

Activity description: The class will be divided into small groups of three or four students. Each group can be assigned a color of the cards to retrieve. The teacher will distribute a series of brown paper bags around the area. Each bag will contain color-coded cards with: clues (for higher level students), terms or cards with drawings of geometric shapes on each one. In the center of the playing area will be a pile of rope pieces of varying lengths. The individual group will be instructed to link elbows or hold hands and utilize a specific loco-motor skill to retrieve one card of their color from a bag and then proceed to the pile of rope pieces and select on piece of rope. They will then return to their starting location and use the piece of rope to design the geometric form described on the card on the ground. Once they have completed that particular task they use the next loco-motor skill (listed on the card) to retrieve a card from the next bag and another piece of rope. This continues until they have gone to each individual bag one time or the teacher determines the activity is completed. The teacher can then compare each group's results or allow the groups to compare each other's results.

Equipment requirements: Color-coded cards with shapes or clues written on each one. Enough paper bags to hold the cards. A sufficient number of pieces of rope to construct the geometric shapes required.

Teacher's notes:

Shape Up!

Focus: Students will cooperate to form geometric shapes using their bodies.

Summary: Students will use their knowledge of geometric shapes to form the appropriate design with the bodies or pathways of travel of their group.

Success criteria: The students will be familiar with various geometric shapes from their work in class. They must call on their experience to construct these shapes using either their bodies or their movements to demonstrate the shape to the class.

Activity diagram: The area required will need only be large enough to allow the groups to have space enough to demonstrate their individual shapes. If loco-motor skills are to be utilized then the area may need to be larger.

Activity description: The teacher will have a series of 3 X 5 cards with the names of the geometric shapes written on them. These will be randomly given to the groups of students and they will be requested to demonstrate the shapes either by using their bodies to represent the shape or by using a loco-motor skill to demonstrate the shape via their pathways. The remainder of the class will then attempt to guess which geometric shape they are representing.

Equipment required: A series of 3 X 5 cards with various geometric shapes written on them.

Teacher's notes:

Smart Steps

Focus: Loco-motor movements and basic mathematic sentences are utilized in a review activity.

Summary: Students will utilize the operations of addition, multiplication and subtraction to perform simple computations while engaged in loco-motor skills.

Success criteria: The students must be familiar with the basic operations of addition, subtraction and multiplication before they can attempt this activity. They must also be capable of performing the operations without paper and pencil.

Activity diagram: Adequate space must be allotted between stations for the movement of the students while performing random loco-motor skills without contact. The size of the students and the number in the class must also be of concern.

Activity description: Students will be told to select and go to the station number card corresponding to their selected number. There should be enough numbers so that no more than one student is at each station or number. Each time the teacher gives a new operation and number they should also suggest a new loco-motor skill to be used to move to the next station. The teacher should begin with basic addition and subtraction sentences and then move on to more complex operations if the students are capable.

Equipment required: The number stations cards.

Teachers' notes:

Take the Money and Run

Focus: Review of denominations of coins in a random loco-motor activity.

Summary: The students will utilize their knowledge of different denominations of coins to determine the appropriate number in response to a given task.

Success criteria: Students will utilize their knowledge of money and how to "make change" to address the specific situations.

Activity diagram: The area required can be either an open area or if the required movements are appropriate the classroom could be used in the activity.

Activity description: The students will be given a task such as skipping around cones or markers, and the teacher will read a statement for the students to respond to which will determine the appropriate number of times a student should perform the task. Examples of the statements would be:
·   Skip around the number of markers which would equal the number of quarters in $2.75
·   Slide in-between the number of pairs of cones, which would equal the number of dimes in $.60
·   Jog around the outside of the square one time for each nickel in a quarter
·   Hop around the markers, which would total the pennies in a dime, etc.

Equipment required: Dependent upon the requirements of the activity and the space available. If the teacher wishes to be creative they may use a number of different types of markers and allow the variety to enter into the specific tasks for the students...skip around only the correct number of blue markers...etc.

Teacher's notes:

Miscellaneous

Circle the Circle

Focus: A concentric circle formation will be used for a review tool of any area of the curriculum.

Summary: The students will answer questions and review a portion of the curriculum in pairs while progressing from station to station in a circular fashion.

Success criteria: Students will be prepared to answer questions, recite spelling of vocabulary words, etc. depending upon the portion of the curriculum selected by the teacher.

Activity diagram: The teacher will designate an area large enough to accommodate the number of pairs of students in the class and the utilization of desired loco-motor skills for movement from station to station.

Activity description: The teacher will layout a series of stations in circular or random fashion with numbers on each so the students will be able to anticipate their rotation sequence. At each station the teacher will place a card or series of cards with a questions and the answer on them for the students to select. Two students moving in opposite directions will come to the station at the same time. One student will be designated as the questioner and the other will be the respondent. (At the even number stations the group moving clockwise will be the questioners and at the odd numbered stations they will be the respondents.) The questioner will select a card and follow the directions: ask for the spelling of a vocabulary word, give the name of a state and ask for its capital, give a mathematics sentence and wait for the answer, etc. If the answer is incorrect they give their partner another chance and then provide the correct answer. If the correct answer is given then they wait for the instruction from the teacher to use the suggested loco-motor skill to move to the next station in their prescribed sequence and direction.

Equipment required: The station numbers of designations, the series of question/answer cards for each station.

Teacher's notes:

Fact Finders

Focus: An activity that can be used to review any portion of the curriculum using a tag game format.

Summary: The student will be a member of a team that will exchange facts concerning a specific topic in a tag game type format.

Success criteria: This will be a review activity for areas of the curriculum. The students will need to be prepared to provide the correct information when asked a specific question.

Activity diagram: The teacher must select a space large enough to allow for freedom of movement in selected loco-motor skills without fear of collision.

Activity description: The students will be divided into teams, the number of which will be dependent upon the information to be reviewed and the number of questions prepared by the teacher. Each player will be given a color-coded pinnie that will designate his or her team. There will be a group of color-coded tubes that contain a card with specific questions to be reviewed. The information can be vocabulary words, facts about specific curricular content, etc. One team (color) will be selected to be "taggers" by the teacher. The "taggers" will attempt to tag members of any other team. When a player is tagged they must spell the word, answer the question, etc. selected by the "tagger" from the card in the tube. If the answer is correct then the "tagger" must attempt to tag another player. If they are incorrect in their response then the ""tagger" reads or recites the correct response, gives the tube to the tagged student and returns to the game. The new "tagger" returns the tube to a central area and takes a tube that corresponds to their team color and attempts to tag another player and repeats the sequences.

Equipment required: Enough tubes and corresponding facts to provide three or four for each color-coded group of "taggers".

Teacher's notes:

Get Together

Focus: Students will establish a consistent partner and small group recognition for future activities.

Summary: Students will develop a consistent recognition of individuals according to the size of individual groups.

Success criteria: Students must remember who is in their individual group as the number of individuals change. Cooperation will be required among the entire class.

Activity diagram: The area needed for this activity is dependent upon the number of students and the loco-motor skills used by the teacher for change between groupings.

Activity description: The teacher will request that the students find a partner and remember who that individual is throughout the activity. Next students must group themselves in three's and they may not be with their partner in the group. The teacher will request that the class form groups of four and no one may be with anyone who was their partner or in their group of three. This continues up until the class has been at its maximum number.

Equipment required: Paper and pencil for each student initially to write the students names. Eventually they will be committed to memory.

Teacher's notes:

Hackysack   (activity appropriate for any type of sequence or progressive material)

Focus: The students will utilize a developmentally appropriate piece of equipment to kick or volley in the air while reciting some portion of the curriculum in sequence, i.e. times tables, alphabet.

Summary: Students will utilize eye-foot coordination with an appropriate piece of equipment to practice spelling and mathematics skills.

Success criteria: The students will practice their spelling and mathematics skills in preparation for participation in a continuous activity using eye-foot coordination.

Activity diagram: The space required will be determined by the size of the class and the groups selected by the teacher. The utilization of larger regulation size and type equipment will require a larger space for all to participate effectively.

Activity description: The teacher will divide the class into groups of students according to their ability level and the selection of equipment. The class will be given pieces of equipment (balloons or balls) to use in participation as their ability level dictates. A balloon is suggested initially to ensure success since it moves very slowly. The teacher will then call out either a vocabulary word that is to be spelled; a number to be counted up to or one or the multiplication times tables to recite. The group of students may use any part of their bodies to keep the balloon (or ball) up in the air while counting, spelling or reciting the correct responses in sequence. Each time an individual contacts the balloon (or ball) in a sequence or at random they call out only the next letter or number in response to the teacher suggested problem. Students continue to spell or recite the answer as many times as possible until the teacher call out the next problem. If the balloon (ball) hits the floor then the group begins again from where they left off in their sequence.

Equipment required: Appropriate curricular material questions or vocabulary, balloons or balls.

Teacher's notes:

Hot Potato

Focus: Students will use a toss and catch activity to review curricular material determined by the teacher.

Summary: Students will utilize tossing and catching skills to review a portion of the curriculum by responding appropriately to questions posed by the teacher. This will serve as a form of review for material that the students have previously covered within the context of the curriculum.

Activity diagram: The teacher will select an appropriate size open area for partners to toss the ball, beanbag or object back and forth successfully.

Activity description: Student will stand a comfortable distance apart and they will toss and catch an appropriate piece of equipment back and forth until the teacher signals to stop. Upon the signal to stop the teacher will either choose the partner with or without the object and they must answer the question, spell the vocabulary word, etc. If the answer offered by the student responding is incorrect then their partner will offer an alternative and hopefully correct response. The teacher may randomly call on partners for the correct response. When the correct answer is given the partners separate and look for a new partner and begin to toss and catch again. If the teacher is concerned they may required that students not have the same partner a second time during the activity.

Equipment required: Balls, beanbags or objects appropriate to the ability level of the students.

Teacher's notes:.

Musical Months

Focus: Review of the sequence of months in the year will be performed after random exchange of month cards.

Summary: Students will demonstrate recognition of the months of the year and the relative position of each one in the appropriate sequence.

Success criteria: The students will be familiar with the proper sequence of the months of the year and capable of reading each of the names.

Activity diagram: The students will need sufficient space to move freely using the designated loco-motor skill without contact.

Activity description: Each student will be given a card with the name of a month on it. The students will also be told to use a specific loco-motor skill while moving around the play area exchanging their cards with whomever they meet at random. The teacher can either use music in the background (similar to a musical chairs concept) or let the students move freely without any background sounds. Upon the stoppage of the music or on a given signal from the teacher the students look for the group with the same color cards and arrange themselves in the appropriate order. This can be repeated a number of times until the teacher is satisfied with the student response to the activity.

Equipment required: Any type of music box can be used. The appropriate number of color-coded laminated cards with the names of the months of the year printed on them.

Teacher's notes:

Olympic Review

Focus: A basic three-student relay configuration is used for reviewing content from the curriculum.

Summary: The students will use groups of two or three to review a portion of the curriculum while performing a designated loco-motor skill.

Success criteria: The students must be familiar with the information to be reviewed and have a working knowledge of how to utilize it relative to the rules established by the teacher.

Activity diagram: The class will need an area large enough to accommodate groups of three moving back and forth with the selected loco-motor skill.

Activity description: Each group of three students will receive a series of review cards. One student will stand on one side of the playing area and their two teammates will be positioned on the other side. When the teacher has designated the appropriate loco-motor skill, the signal is given and one of the two students will move across the playing area carrying the series of cards for their team and stop in front of their teammate. The student carrying the series of cards will hold them up in a fanned position with the answer side toward them and their teammate will select a question from the group. When the card is chosen the student holding the series of cards will ask the appropriate question and the teammate will attempt to answer the question. If an incorrect answer is offered they have a second chance at the correct response. If the incorrect answer is given again the holder tells the teammate the correct answer. When the answer is correct the cards are given to their teammates and they switch roles. The teammate returns to the other side using the prescribed loco-motor skill and asks the other teammate to select a card and continues the process until the teacher stops the activity and has the groups switch series of cards.

Equipment required: Enough series of cards for the class to have at least six to eight cards per group of three. These can have any type of curricular review information on them.

Teacher's notes:

Out and Around

Focus: Review activity that allows students to work together to answer questions from any content area.

Summary: The students will cooperate in pairs to solve the problems set forth by the teacher while performing a loco-motor skill.

Success criteria: Students must be capable of following directions and cooperate in pairs to solve problems and perform a loco-motor skill.

Activity diagram: The space required can be adjusted according to the size of the class and the desired activity level for the students. Generally a space of 10- to 15-yards square will be sufficient to provide adequate activity for the participants.

Activity description: The students will find a partner these can be switched numerous times during the activity at the discretion of the teacher. The partners will link elbows and stand on a line that is the outer boundary for the playing area. The teacher will request that the students begin to perform a loco-motor skill around the activity area. The teacher will then ask the pairs to think of a response to a given statement. The statements will concern some portion of the general classroom curriculum. Examples of these statements could be:

> Think of:
>> a word that contains the letters "am" (came, frame, game, etc.)
>> something that comes in pairs (gloves, socks, shoes etc.)
>> a place where people work (supermarket, factory, shoe store, etc.)
>> how many even numbers are in today's date
>> how many ounces are in a pound
>> the product of 4 X 9, etc.

When the pair has thought of an answer they may begin to circle markers or cones that are randomly placed around the activity area continuing to use the loco-motor skill. They count how many markers they circle using the loco-motor skill before the teacher makes the next statement. Each time a new statement is provided they must return to their starting position on the outer boundary before re-entering the activity area and solving the next statement that the teacher calls out. The focus of the activity is cooperation in solving the problem or statement and not the number of markers circled. The teacher should not ask for a result or count from the pairs. The loco-motor skill should be performed at a comfortable level of intensity to allow the participants to continue.

Equipment required: A list of curricular questions.

Teacher's notes:

Sequence Scramble

Focus: Students will be given a card corresponding to a specific sequence and on a signal the will arrange themselves appropriately.

Summary: Students will cooperate to perform designated loco-motor movements while arranging themselves in a proper sequence determined by the cards selected.

Success criteria: The students will understand the proper sequence of number letters or symbols in order that they may arrange themselves correctly in lines.

Activity diagram: Any large open area will be sufficient for this activity.

Activity description: The students will be divided into appropriate size groups; 26 for the alphabet, 12 for times tables, etc. The teacher will designate which loco-motor skill the students are to utilize as they move around the area and get into the appropriate sequence. One of the cardholders will be designated as the leader. That individual student will be holding a card that is either at the beginning or the end of the sequence and all the students must line up while performing the loco-motor skill in their proper position. The group continues to move until the teacher signals and the students return their cards and receive a new series of cards and begin a new loco-motor skill. This activity can be made more difficult by assigning the leader to a letter or number that falls in the middle of a sequence and the remainder of the students must determine which is the beginning and which is the end of the line. There can be more than one sequence being formed at one time by having each leaders perform a different loco-motor skills which can be designated on the sequence cards and the students must recognize their loco-motor skill and get in line in the appropriate sequence.

Equipment required: Series of cards that make up sequences and designate loco-motor skills to be utilized.

Teacher's notes:

Skip It

Focus: The activity of rope jumping will be used to review sequence type curricular content, i.e. times tables, spelling words, etc.

Summary: The students will utilize their skill in rope jumping to address the specific tasks set by the teacher.

Success criteria: Students will use their mathematics, spelling, or any other progressive sequence skills in combination with their rope jumping ability to respond to the teachers' tasks.

Activity diagram: The area required should be sufficient to provide each students adequate space to swing their jump rope over their heads without interference with another student.

Activity description: The students will each receive a rope to skip with and be instructed to find their own space. The students will scatter randomly around the activity area and await the direction of the teacher. The students should be allowed to practice their technique and adjust their spacing according to the flight of their ropes. When the teacher is satisfied that there will be no problems caused by the rotation of the individual ropes they will provide a task for the students. Each task can be either continuous, such as repeating the three times table to twelve with one jump for each number or discontinuous, such as stop after you jump enough times to spell *Mississippi*. The jumping and the tasks should fit the curriculum of the students.

Equipment required: One jump rope for each child. If the teacher wishes to challenge the children then they may wish to provide long ropes for multiple jumpers.

Teacher's notes:

Music

Listen, Watch and Move

Focus: Music tempo and basic reading and recognition skills are used to review concepts.

Summary: Students will demonstrate their ability to read and respond to the words and phrases presented by the teacher and attempt to perform movements to the underlying beat of the music.

Success criteria: The students will be prepared to listen to a piece of music and determine the underlying beat and perform some type of movement with their hands to the beat. They must also be capable of reading a series of words or distinguishing movements that are symbolized on flash cards and perform the associated loco-motor skills.

Activity diagram: The area required for this activity will be determined by the size of the class and the age and size of the students. The teacher will need to provide adequate space for freedom of movement without contact between the students while performing the various loco-motor skills.

Activity description: The teacher will select and play a piece of music that has an easily distinguishable beat. The students will be asked to perform a response with their hands such as clapping or snapping their fingers to determine the beat of the music. The teacher will then display a series of flash cards that represent various loco-motor skills and the students will demonstrate the appropriate response. The teacher will now incorporate the music with the loco-motor skill and allow the students to challenge themselves to find the correct tempo for their movement to the beat of the music. This will be practiced before the students are asked to respond to the flash cards randomly displayed to the class.

Equipment required: The teacher must be careful to select appropriate music that displays a definitive underlying beat that the students can readily distinguish. Flash cards should be large and easily read (for younger children they can be pictures of children performing the movements).

Teacher's notes:

Time Travel

Focus: The teacher will employ cooperative group problem solving to construct movements and follow tempo to a variety of music selections.

Summary: Students will cooperate in small groups to perform movements that match the tempo of music provided by the teacher.

Success criteria: Students should have demonstrated the ability to distinguish among a variety of music forms and tempos in cognitive activities initially. Students should also have had the opportunity to engage in free form body movements to a variety of music tempos.

Activity diagram: The students will need an adequate area or floor space to freely engage in a variety of loco-motor and non-loco-motor movement patterns.

Activity description: The teacher will request that the class break-up in the desired number of students per group. Each group will hear the same instruction regarding the function of its' members. Instructions could include: that the group must move around the provided area with specific body parts in contact with the floor surface, only a certain number of feet may be in contact with the floor at one time, arms must be kept above their shoulders, etc. The group of students should then devise some type of movement that meets the suggested criteria. The teacher will put on a specific piece of music for which the students must identify the tempo and adjust their selected movements to be in unison with that particular tempo. The teacher may change the groups, the tempo or the specifications of the movement parameters at any time to further engage the students.

Activity description: A variety of music selections that are familiar with the students and ones to which they enjoy listening.

Teacher's notes:

Science

Any Old Leaf Will Do

Focus: Review of characteristics associated with trees and shrubbery local to students.

Summary: Students will demonstrate knowledge of the different types of trees and shrubbery along with the corresponding colors and characteristics of the leaves in a tag game activity.

Success criteria: The students must study the colors, shapes, tree of origin or some other distinguishing characteristic before they participate in this activity.

Activity diagram: This activity can be played in either an end-to-end formation or a square depending upon the space available and the size of the class. Students will be requested to use a suggested loco-motor skill to cross either from one end to the other or from side to side.

Activity description: The teacher will break the students up into the appropriate number of groups according to the subject matter. This may be fall colors, leave shapes or structures, leaf colors, etc. whatever is being studied in the curriculum. Students will each receive a leaf or the construction paper representation of the leaf to begin the activity. Students will be assigned a loco-motor skill to utilize while moving around the area exchanging their leaves with any student from another group. The teacher will give a signal and the students will move together and compare the leaves that each one has brought back to the group. The teacher can provide paper and pencil for the students to list characteristics that they can recall from class discussions. The activity will be repeated and at the end the teacher can review specific information for each type of leaf included.

Equipment required: Colored leaves or construction paper leaves. Provide paper and pencils for the students to list the characteristics from class discussions.

Teacher's notes:

Earth, Wind, Fire & Water

Focus: The skills of tossing and catching will be used in conjunction with review of science curriculum materials.

Summary: The students will recall elements of the curriculum that are specifically associated with class science concepts to be used in this toss and catch game.

Success criteria: The students must be familiar with and capable of recalling specific information regarding the science curriculum.

Activity diagram: The students will require sufficient space to toss and catch the types of balls provided for the activity. The space should allow for individual differences and challenges for each pair of students.

Activity description: Each pair of students will be provided with a developmentally appropriate piece of equipment to toss and catch at the selected distance. The teacher will determine a specific signal and the student, who has the ball in their possession or is about to catch the ball, if it is in the air when the signal is given, will answer the questions posed by the teacher. The teacher will have a prepared list of questions that come from the class science curriculum. These questions should ask the students to identify some aspect of the four elements of earth, wind, fire or water. If the student is unsure of their answer their partner may assist them. The object of the activity is for the pairs to score as many points as possible within the given time of the activity. The teacher should be available to mediate answers that are controversial.

Equipment required: A sufficient number of balls or objects for each pair of students. A list of questions directly related to the science curriculum covered in class.

Teacher's notes:

Ecology Tag

Focus: A tag game format will be used to review the concept of litter and the effect on the ecology.

Summary: The students will demonstrate the principle of recycling in a tag game format.

Success criteria: The students must be capable of safely participating a tag game and following directions.

Activity diagram: The students will need sufficient space for a chase and flee type activity with room for three hula hoops without collisions or tripping over the equipment.

Activity description: Each of the players will have a flag belt or two scarves tucked into their belts or pockets. The teacher will designate three players to be the "recyclers." The "recyclers" will wear green colored pinnies and have a green piece of cloth in the center back of their pants. Each of these will stand inside one hoop that is their safe area. Two or more players will then be designated the "litter bugs," they will attempt to tag the other players. The "litter bugs" will also be given a colored pinnie (other than green) to carry which is easily visible and one long piece of similar colored cloth to tuck into the center back of their pants. If a player, other than the "recyclers," can grab and secure the piece of cloth from the "litter bug" without having one of their scarves stolen, then they change roles with a "litter bug." After a "litter bug" has tagged a player by stealing their scarf they return the scarf and attempt to tag additional players. If a player has had a scarf stolen they must stand still with their feet spread apart until a "recycler" can come out and pass the green cloth or pinnie between their legs without having their scarf stolen. If they are successful then both players switch roles and continue to play. If the "litter bug" steals a "recyclers" green colored tail from the back then both players must switch roles and continue to play. The game continues and the teacher can change the players' role at any time.

Equipment required: Flag belts or enough scarves for each student to have two, three or more pieces of green cloth and green colored pinnies or T-shirts for the "recyclers," two or more other colored pinnies or T-shirts and pieces of cloth for the "litter bugs," three or more hula hoops for the safe areas.

Teacher's notes:

Fill in the Blank

Focus: The class science notes will be reviewed in a group activity utilizing stations corresponding to specific areas of the curriculum.

Summary: The students will utilize loco-motor skills to travel around the area correctly spelling the answer to a science related question.

Success criteria: Students must be familiar with the science related information utilized by the teacher.

Activity diagram: The area should be large and unobstructed. There should be sufficient wall or window space to allow the teacher to tape the stations and letters to the surfaces for the students to move around. Stations should be randomly spaced around the room with letters of the alphabet in-between each station.

Activity description: The teacher will establish a number of stations according to the number of students in the class and the size of the groups they wish to use. It is suggested that pairs or threes would be best for maximum participation. Each group would start at a station and rotate around to all the stations by the end of the activity. Each station will include a sheet of paper with a statement concerning some portion of the curriculum with one critical word left out. These words should be the focus of the student activity. The group will discuss the answer and then when they reach a decision they will link elbows or hold hands and utilize the loco-motor skill assigned at the bottom of the sheet to move around the room from letter to letter spelling the answer to the blank space. When they have finished they will return to the original station and lift up the answer card flap to see if they were accurate in their spelling of the answer. Once they have finished that station they move on to the next station in sequence and repeat the process. This continues until they have completed all the stations or the teacher feels that they have had enough activity.

Equipment required: Station cards with statements and blanks along with an answer flap and alphabet cards for the walls.

Teacher's notes:

Match Tag

Focus: A tag game will be the vehicle for a review of the class information in the science curriculum related to pictures and terminology.

Summary: Students will utilize their knowledge of various portions of the curriculum to recognize and match pictures with the names of the item in a tag game format.

Success criteria: Students must be familiar with the pictures and names of the materials used in the game and are prepared to match them at the end of the activity.

Activity diagram: The area required will need to permit a chase and flee type activity without fear of collision.

Activity description: The teacher will distribute flag belts or scarves to each student and equally divide the number of cards among the students in a random fashion. The class will be divided into teams and provided with pinnies to distinguish the teams. The teacher will designate a loco-motor skill to be utilized during the activity. On the signal from the teacher the students will attempt to capture flags/scarves from members of the other teams. If a flag/scarf is captured then the player who captured the flag/scarf returns the flag/scarf and is given the top card from the other players pile. Students who are returning flags/scarves or exchanging cards may not have their flags/scarves stolen. [If necessary you may designate an exchange area that is a safe zone.] When the exchange is completed they return to the activity and continue to capture flags/scarves from other players. At the end of the activity the groups get together and compare cards to see how many pairs they have captured. The activity can be repeated or the teacher can use the pairs secured as the beginning of the group discussion and review of the material.

Equipment required: Colored pinnies to distinguish the teams, pairs of cards for distribution to the players, markers to designate the exchange zone, scarves or flag belts.

Teacher's notes:

Now & Then

Focus: Characteristics of trees and leaves will be reviewed in a partner activity.

Summary: Students will utilize their knowledge of trees and their individual leaves to participate in a cooperative activity to find their corresponding partners.

Success criteria: The students will be involved in a unit of study surrounding the phases or changes of the seasons and its effect on the trees' foliage. They will need to identify the leaves in their different stages.

Activity diagram: An area for participation will be needed to allow for freedom of movement in the chosen loco-motor skill and sufficient room for an exchange zone to select the new leaves.

Activity description: The students will be instructed to utilize a loco-motor skill appropriate for the play area available. They will each be given a variety of leaves that will correspond to another leaf that represents another season or phase of growth for a particular tree. The students will move around the play area attempting to find their partner with the corresponding leaf and then both partners will return to the exchange area and select two new leaves. When the students exchange leaves they must return to the play area and find another partner with a corresponding leaf, it should not be the same partner again. The loco-motor skill can be changed as often as necessary to prevent fatigue and boredom. The greater the variety of leaves the longer the students will have to move around before finding their partner and returning to the exchange zone.

Equipment required: Pairs of leaves that represent different phases of the growth cycle or seasons of the trees. The more varieties of tree the better to keep the activity interesting and active.

Teacher's notes:

Orbit Ball

Focus: A tag game will be the vehicle for a review of information related to the solar system.

Summary: Students will demonstrate an understanding of the relationship among the sizes of the planets in the universe and specific information about them.

Success criteria: The students will acquire a working knowledge of the planets and their relative size. They will use their information background in a game format.

Activity diagram: The space required will need to facilitate the type of loco-motor skill utilized and the size of class participating. An area that is free of obstructions and has a flat surface would be best suited for this activity.

Activity description: The teacher will distribute various balls that represent the various planets. The students who have the balls will be considered "taggers" initially. The teacher will prescribe a loco-motor skill for the class to use when moving around the playing area. The students with the planets must tag another student with the ball. When a student is tagged with the planet ball the "tagger" will ask the question which is on top of the planet pile they are carrying. After the "tagger" has tagged enough students to ask all the questions in their pile the last student tagged becomes the new "tagger". The activity continues until the teacher feels satisfied with participation.

Equipment required: The teacher must design and label the appropriate number of different size balls. Sets of planet information cards.

Teacher's notes:

Planet Scramble

Focus: Random loco-motor skills will provide movement for the students as they review information concerning the solar system.

Summary: The students will utilize information concerning the Solar System and their ability to spell the names of the planets while using a specific loco-motor skill.

Success criteria: Students will recall the names of the planets and their position relative to the sun to place them in proper position with the remainder of the class.

Activity diagram: The area required will need sufficient space for the groups of students to move around in a circular formation using the designated loco-motor skill. Preferably this would be an outdoor area or an area as large as a gymnasium.

Activity description: The teacher will divide the class into groups. The teacher will then distribute a series of cards to each individual or group. Each series will contain all ten planets (sun included) with the letters of the name scrambled. The cards will also contain information concerning the type of loco-motor skill to be used. The group or individual will unscramble the letter on the card and determine the name of the appropriate planet and then use the suggested loco-motor skill to circle the sun in their position relative to the solar system. When they have completed all ten planets in their proper positions they should all be moving around the sun using the loco-motor skill.

Equipment required: Series of cards with the names of the planets scrambled on them.

Teacher's notes:

Planet Tag

Focus: A tag game format is utilized to distribute and exchange cards that represent the planets of the solar system.

Summary: The students will utilize their knowledge of the solar system and avoid being tagged in a chase and flee activity.

Success criteria: Students will be required to utilize specific knowledge and information concerning the solar system and its individual planets.

Activity diagram: A large open area in which the students can move freely without fear of collision while utilizing the assigned loco-motor skill.

Activity description: The teacher will have a series of cards (at least one for each of the planets of the solar system) and then will designate two, three or more students (depending on the size of the class) to be "taggers". The students that are "taggers" must chase the remainder of the class using a prescribed loco-motor skill. The remainder of the class will attempt to avoid be tagged. When a student is tagged they must determine which planet the letter on the "taggers" card represents by answering the question on the back of the card. If the student tagged cannot answer the question then they take the card to the teacher to get a new one and they become a "tagger" and attempt to tag another class member. The game can also be played so that whenever a player is tagged they must take the card to the teacher and switch for another card whether they know the answer or not.

Equipment required: A series of laminated cards that represent the solar system with question on one side and the first letter of the planet on the other.

Teacher's notes:

Polluted Pond

Focus: The concept of pollution will be reviewed as it relates to waterfowl or natural resources associated with bodies of water.

Summary: The students will participate in an activity designed to demonstrate the concept of pollution and the effect on waterfowl in a pond.

Success criteria: The students will have some knowledge of the concept of pollution and the effect on the environment.

Activity diagram: The space required must have a smooth flat surface upon which the beanbags will slide freely.

Activity description: The teacher will divide the class into three or four groups. One group will be placed in the center of the area. Also in the center of the playing area will be a series of cups or objects. The students on the outside will be provided with beanbags which they will slide using their feet. The outside students will attempt to knock down the cups/objects by sliding the beanbags into the center area. The group of students in the center may block the beanbags that are slid into the center and slide them back out. After a given period of time, determined by the teacher, the activity will stop and there will be a count of the number of cups/objects that are knocked over. These can be representative of ducks or waterfowl that have died due to the pollution caused by the beanbags. The number of beanbags in the center can also be representative of more dead waterfowl (such as; one dead duck for each five bean bags). This can then be the genesis for discussions on the effects of pollution. The teacher can then change groups and repeat the activity and generate further discussions.

Equipment required: Bean bags, cups or objects that can stand on end.

Teacher's notes:

Prehistoric Tag

Focus: Using a tag game format, students will review the names and pronunciation of a variety of dinosaurs.

Summary: The students will utilize their knowledge of the names of various dinosaurs while using a loco-motor skill to avoid being tagged.

Success criteria: The students must be familiar with a number of the names of various dinosaurs.

Activity diagram: A large open area in which the students can move freely without fear of collision while utilizing the assigned loco-motor skill.

Activity description: The teacher will randomly select two or three students to be "taggers" for the first round. The "taggers" will wear or carry a pinnie to distinguish them from the remainder of the class. Each student will also carry a card with the name of one type of dinosaur printed on it. When the teacher has assigned the appropriate loco-motor skill and the students are spaced around the area they will give the signal to begin. "Taggers" will chase the other students around the area and attempt to tag them. Once a "tagger" has successfully tagged a student they will hold up their card in front of them so the student who was tagged can read it. If the student can correctly pronounce the name of the dinosaur then they return to the game and the "tagger" attempts to find another student to tag. If they are not able to read the name of the dinosaur then they take the pinnie and become a "tagger." The teacher may change "taggers" numerous times during the activity to keep the student's role rotating. To increase the cognitive demands of the activity the teacher can print an important fact concerning the specific type of dinosaur on the back of the card which the tagged student must recite to avoid becoming the "tagger." The curriculum and student interest will be the best gauge for this approach.

Equipment required: The teacher must produce enough cards for the students to each have one card and extras to rotate into the activity. Provide pinnies for the students to wear or carry.

Teacher's notes:

Snakes and Mice

Focus: A tag game format is used to provide a simulation of the food chain.

Summary: The students will graph and analyze the results of a tag game as it relates to the concept of the food chain and survival in the animal world.

Success criteria: The students must be capable of playing a tag game and following directions and graphing the results of the game.

Activity diagram: The students will need a space long and wide enough to allow them to cross back and forth with room to stop and change direction without collisions or hitting the walls.

Activity description: The teacher will randomly choose two or more students to be the snakes. They will stand in the middle of the playing area. The remainder of the class will stand on one side of the playing area and wait the teachers signal to cross to the other side. All players will use a designated loco-motor skill. The snakes will attempt to tag one and only one mouse crossing to the other side and that player becomes a snake. At the end of each round the students count how many snakes and mice are left. These numbers are recorded and eventually graphed. If a snake does not catch a mouse as they cross the playing area then since they have no food they die and become a mouse for the next round. After a number of rounds the results are graphed and the class will discuss the way in which the graph relates to the food chain concept.

Equipment required: Pencil, paper and graph paper.

Teachers' notes:

Solar System Scramble

Focus: A tag game format is utilized to review information concerning the solar system.

Summary: The students will utilize their knowledge of the location of the planets in a game of tag.

Success criteria: The student must be aware of the relative positions of the planets in the solar system when called upon to arrange him or herself correctly.

Activity diagram: The area needed will depend on the size of the class and the age of the students. The teacher can utilize various loco-motor skills to limit the level of participation.

Activity description: The teacher will randomly distribute the appropriate number of spheres or balls to individual students. When the teacher has assigned the desired loco-motor skill to be utilized by the class they will give the signal to begin. Students with the balls or spheres will attempt to tag other students with the spheres or balls. A student who tags another student should yell out the name of the planet they are carrying. When a student is tagged they then take the ball or sphere and move to tag another student ("no tag backs"). After a given period of time determined by the teacher a signal is given and whichever students have the spheres or balls must line up according to their relative correct position in the solar system. After the correct positions are established the signal to resume the tag game is given and the process is repeated as many times as the teacher feels comfortable with the outcome.

Equipment required: An appropriate number of spheres or balls that are either labeled with the planet names of are chosen according to the relative sizes of the planets.

Teacher's notes:

Social Studies

Capture the Revolutionary Flag

Focus: To examine the concept of the Revolutionary war and the use of troops in battle.

Summary: The students will participate in a tag game design to simulate the diversity in the American revolutionary war.

Success criteria: The students will be capable of playing a tag game and following directions during the activity. The activity will be designed to depict the tactics and movements of the armies in the material studied.

Activity diagram: The space required will allow the freedom of movement using designated loco-motor skills without fear of collision among the participants.

Activity description: Each student will be given a flag belt or scarves to tuck into their pants or pockets. The teacher will divide the class by having the students count off by threes. This will allow the teacher to have number one start by being the Colonial soldiers and numbers two and three partner up to be the British soldiers. Numbers two and three will link their elbows together. These pairs of students will represent the British army. Each team will be assigned to one side of the playing area to begin the game. The teacher will set up four cones with beanbags balanced on the tops behind each team. The teacher will give the signal to begin. The object of the game is to get the four beanbags from the other team and return them to your home base (hula hoops) without being tagged (having one of your flags/scarves stolen). If a player or pair is tagged (has their flags/scarves stolen) in the opposing teams side of the playing area then they must return the bean bag to the cone where they found it and return to their side of the playing area before they may attempt to cross over and steal another bean bag. This continues until the teacher is satisfied and then the numbers change roles until each team has had a chance to be the Colonial Army. The students should now discuss why it made a difference who was the Colonial Army and what did that difference represent in the war?

Equipment required: Two hula-hoops for home bases, eight cones and eight beanbags. Markers are required to signify the centerline of the playing area, flag belts or scarves for each participant.

Teacher's notes:

Guerrilla Tactics

Focus: Tactics of various wars over history can be discussed as a result of game like format.

Summary: Students will engage in an activity that is intended to replicate a specific type of Guerrilla conflict in which the roles of the participants simulate a disparity.

Success criteria: There is no requirement other than the ability to slide or roll the objects in an underarm motion at a target. Familiarity with some type of historic conflict would provide a context for the activity.

Activity diagram: The space needs to be large enough to accommodate the number of students and the projection of objects at targets. Half a standard size basketball court should be more than adequate and may be too large depending on the size of the targets.

Activity description: The teacher will set up boundaries for the entire activity. Then the teacher will set up an inside boundary which should be approximately one quarter the size of the total area. [This inside area can be in a corner or against the side of the outer boundary at the teachers' discretion. Having played the game a couple of times the teacher can change the location of this area to meet different discussion objectives.] The size of the teams can be determined by the teacher to meet discussion objectives. The one team may only move inside the small area. The other team may move anywhere inside the larger area. Targets (cups, bottles, bowling pins, cones, etc.) should be set up and equally distributed between both areas. Each student should receive at least one object (ball, bean bag, etc.) at the beginning. When the teacher gives the signal the students may only project the objects at the targets controlled by the opposing team. When a ball or beanbag goes outside the designated area only a player from the target area may retrieve it. The teacher will end that round of the game after a designated time period or when one team has knocked down all the targets. Players should switch roles and play the game again with similar restriction. After each student has had the opportunity to be in both roles the teacher should discuss the issues surrounding each role and the advantages and disadvantages of each situation. This can be related to the American Revolution, Colonial Indian Wars, Vietnam War, or any other conflict in which the rules of engagement demonstrated a disparity. This discussion can lead to many issues that concerning war in general and perceptions of fairness and winning.

Equipment required: Pinnies to designate the team members. Balls or bean bags to be used to knock down objects. Bowling pins, cups, bottles, cones or some other objects to be used as targets and boundary markers for the designation of the one teams area.

Teacher's notes:

Presidential Line-up

Focus: Specific information concerning past and present Presidents will be reviewed.

Summary: Students will utilize information concerning the Presidents of the United States and their terms of office in a loco-motor skills activity.

Success criteria: Students must be familiar with all the information included in the activity relative to each of the Presidents.

Activity diagram: Students will need area in which they can freely move about using a designated loco-motor skill in a type of chase and flee activity

Activity description: Each student will be given a card with information concerning a specific President written on it. The card may have the name, birthplace, or any other piece of relevant information listed on it. The piece of information that is missing will be that which the teacher wants the students to remember, such as; sequence in the White House or political party etc. The students will randomly move around the room using the designated loco-motor skill and will exchange cards whenever the teacher calls for a change. On a given signal the teacher will have the students line up according to a specific criteria. The designated criteria could be sequence in the White House, grouping by political party, alphabetically, etc. The information on the cards and the groupings are dependent upon the teacher and the curriculum.

Equipment required: Sufficient cards for the students to exchange while moving around the room. Cards could be duplicated or in a series of multiples depending upon the depth of information being covered.

Teacher's notes:

Take 'em Home

Focus: Determining the native homelands for a variety of animals while using loco-motor skills to move around a designated area.

Summary: The students will utilize a designated loco-motor skill to return a series of pictures that represent endangered and indigenous species to their correct homeland.

Success criteria: The students will be able to recognize and name a variety of animals and endangered species from pictures and representations and associate them with their native homelands and the relative continents.

Activity diagram: The students will need an area large enough to utilize the suggested loco-motor skills in an obstacle free environment.

Activity description: The teacher will divide the class into groups of students who will work together "to take the animals home." The activity area will have large posters of either continents or countries on them to represent the native homelands of the animals being studied. Each group will have a starting point or home base. One at a time a student will use the designated loco-motor skill to travel to the center of the room and pick a card which is face down. They will return to their team using the designated loco-motor skill and show the card to their team so that they can determine to which poster the card should be taken. After the student leaves "to take the animal home" the next student in the group goes to get another card to bring back to the group for review. This continues until all the cards are gone or the teacher decides to stop the activity. The class then reviews each of the posters to see if the animals were taken to their correct homeland. The activity can be repeated as many times as the teacher feels appropriate. This activity can also incorporate other curricular information; such as: natural rescues, cities, primary exports, etc.

Equipment required: The teacher can utilize the assistance of the students to create a series of cards that have pictures or names of animals that are native to the continents and countries being studied.

Teacher's notes:

Westward Ho

Focus: The concept of westward expansion and the Indian reservations will be depicted in an activity format.

Summary: The students will experience a game scenario designed to simulate the westward expansion of settlers in the early west and utilize follow up discussions to draw analogies to the game participation.

Success criteria: Students will be familiar with the concept of musical chairs and work cooperatively to fulfill their role in the game.

Activity diagram: The space required should allow for freedom of movement in and around the objects set up in the playing area.

Activity description: The class will be divided in half and each group will be given one color of pinnie. One team will be designated as the "Settlers" and the other will be "Native Americans." The teacher will position hoops, carpet squares, poly spots or some other designating surface around the playing area. Inside each of these areas the teacher will place a cone or cup at the beginning of the game. These areas are considered to be the homelands of the "Native Americans" at the beginning of the westward expansion. The teacher will either play some form of music (similar to musical chairs) or simply allow the students to move around until a specific signal is given. When the teacher gives the signal all the students will utilize the designated loco-motor skill to move around the playing area. When the music stops or the signal is given the students move to a position. The restrictions for the selection of a position include: "Native American" players may only occupy positions with cones on them, as many students as necessary are allowed on each position, no position may have two players from opposite teams, after each round the cones are taken from positions occupied by any settlers, unused positions remain as they were at the beginning of the round. The music begins again and the players move around using the designated loco-motor skill until the music stops or the signal is again given to find a position. With each round there will be fewer positions for the "Native Americans" until they have only one for the whole team or possibly none. Switch the students' roles begin the activity again and then end the game with a discussion of how it felt to be the "Native Americans" searching for their own land.

Equipment required: Carpet squares, hoops, ploy spots or some other type of designations, cones or cups as markers, two colors of pinnies.

Teacher's notes

Chapter Six

Creating Your Own Games and Activities

Chapter Overview

This chapter examines the reasons why you would want to modify existing activities. Some of the concepts of developmental appropriateness as well as the individual aspects of activities that may be modified are examined. Steps that can be taken in the actual game or activity modifications are outlined.

Questions to Consider

1. What are the various reasons for modifying activities?

2. What are some of the factors that prevent game or activity modification?

3. What are the three major areas which can be considered when modifying a game or activity?

4. What specific things do you consider in the existing game or activity when attempting to modify it?

5. How closely should the modified game or activity resemble the original one?

Why Create or Modify Your Own Games?

There are a number of great games and activities to be found in a variety of trade books and resources. These activities are fun to participate in and provide a great deal of activity. If this is the case, why should we create or modify activities? There are three reasons to create or modify activities.

First, the game may be developmentally inappropriate for the particular level with which we are working. While the idea of the activity has good potential for providing cognitive skill development, the activity itself may be either too simple or too complex to accomplish this task. In either case, adjustments will have to be made to accommodate the needs of the target group with whom we are working. Second, while a game seems to provide a great deal of activity for all participants, analysis of the activity may reveal that in actuality, only a few are really participating at a high level, while others are not really that involved or spend too much time waiting. Third, the activity, while seeming useful initially, fails to meet our needs. Perhaps the chances of activity failure can be reduced or eliminated, however.

Modifying Your Own Games and Activities

When an activity does not suit our purposes many people see only two choices, use the activity because of the potential enjoyment or don't use the activity at all. There is a third choice, however. We can modify the activity.

Factors That Prevent Activity Modification

Many people who work with children fail to see the modification option because of their respect for the historical background of the activity, their respect for the written word or because they are unsure about how to modify activities.

Historical Perspective

Over the years certain games and activity achieve classic status. Kickball and Circle Dodgeball are two such activities. Classroom teachers, camp counselors and recreation leaders play these activities the same way they have been played for generations. There is a certain way to play these games and tradition prevents many people from even considering changing the format of these activities.

The Written Rule

We have a great respect for the printed word. As such, when we see an activity in a book or magazine, we teach and use the activity exactly as it is described. We follow the rules to the letter and never change any of the format used in the activity. We do not see modification as an option because a "higher authority" (the author) has informed us how an activity should be conducted.

Lack of Knowledge

Finally, people do not modify activities because they just don't know how to go about it. They don't know what to change or how to change it. There is a lack of understanding regarding the components of an activity and the options available that may be utilized to enhance an activity or make it more useful for a given situation.

What Can You Modify?

Now that you are aware that activities can and should be modified as necessary, let's examine the modification process. There are three key components to consider when thinking about activity modification. These are the organism (group using the activity) utilizing the activity, the environment in which the activity is meant to take place and the tasks involved in successfully completing or taking part in the activity (Barrett, et al, 1994).

The Organism

The organism in our case is the child or student. Unfortunately, this element cannot be modified on a day-to-day basis. The students we encounter on any given day are the students or children with whom we must work. While we hope to see change over time, we cannot consider the organism (child) a viable option in activity modification. We still have two remaining options, however. We can still examine and modify the environment or the task.

The Environment

The environment is the setting in which an activity is designed to take place. The most obvious environments are the physical location. Activities can be played indoors or outdoors. Professional athletics has shown us that there is no reason that traditional outdoor activities cannot be moved indoors, however. Football, soccer and lacrosse are such examples. These are not the only environmental considerations.

The size and shape of the area in which a game is played can also be changed to better suit the needs of the participants and the objectives of the activity. Reducing the size of the playing area can accommodate the endurance levels of younger children much more effectively, allowing them to remain active at higher levels for shorter periods of time. Including rest zones or safety areas in activities that allow children to stop and catch their breath if necessary can also accommodate the endurance of level of the children. This allows the child with less endurance to be more successful and remain in the activity.

The size and shape of goals is another consideration for environmental modification. Traditional goals such as baskets or soccer nets, need not be used simply because they are available. A regulation basketball is inappropriate for most elementary level children. Even when lowered to eight feet many children still have difficulty successfully using this goal. In truth, anything can be used as a goal. A spot painted on the wall, a target on the floor, a wastebasket, a plastic cup on the floor or a hula-hoop hung over a basketball basket can all serve as goals. What you can use is only limited by your imagination.

Another environmental factor is the make up of teams. Many activities call for two teams. Teachers see this and naturally respond by splitting the class in two to form the necessary number of teams. Often, however, the activity directions do not say that these teams require a specific number of players on each team. There is nothing to stop you from making four or six teams and playing two or three separate games rather than one big game. This type of change allows more children to be substantively active within the game for longer periods of time. It prevents the more motorically gifted children from taking over the activity further limiting the participation of all players.

The Task

The other part of an activity that can be modified is the task itself. There are a number of task components that can be considered when modifying an activity. In order to better understand this concept, however, you must first understand what a task can be. A task by definition is a piece of work to be done. In many physical education or game type activities the task deals with the final product or terminal outcome; such as the touchdown in football, the run in baseball, the goal in soccer or hockey or the strike in bowling. Closer examination reveals, however, that these final outcomes are the result of a number of smaller tasks that allow the final task to occur. Throwing and kicking with accuracy, striking a thrown object, catching a thrown or struck object and the ability to move efficiently at different speeds and in different directions are a few of the skills required to successfully complete the terminal outcomes of the aforementioned sports. Bearing this in mind, any of these component skills can become the target outcome for an activity, thereby improving the students' ability to perform the component parts of the larger task enhancing the possibilities or success in the larger task.

For example, instead of having students play a game where points are scored for scoring tradition style goals, points could be awarded for completing a prescribed number of accurate passes to different teams members. Running, which is the most common locomotor form used in activities, can be substituted with walking, skipping, galloping or any combination of locomotor movements. Activities can be designed that focus on the process used in the larger sport's context.

Activities designed to focus on throwing, catching, striking or passing are all possible. These activities should not be conducted in a drill type format, however. These activities should use a game-like format. They should have agreed upon set of rules and an observable outcome. Most importantly, though, they should be fun to participate in while providing practice in the desired skill component.

Modifying Activities to Fit a Theme

There may be times when you want an activity to help present or reinforce a particular theme, such as History, Mathematics or Science. While this may take a bit more thought and planning, as seen by examples shown in Chapter Four, it is possible. A few different considerations are involved in this process.

First, as with all activities, identify your objectives. In this case, I have selected **Westward Ho,** an activity that was designed to show the historical impact of the westward expansion of settlers on the Native Americans. The underlying theme was to gradually have the settlers move west while at the same time restricting Native American movement and available area. The activity required "parcels of land" which could gradually be opened up to the advancing settlers as it was denied to the Native Americans. Carpet squares were chosen for this purpose, however, hoops, polyspots or bases would work just as effectively. Next, who could use the specific areas of land was established. Since this activity deals with western expansion, the eastern edge of the land area is identified as the original settler area. The remaining areas are identified as Native

American land and are marked with a cone. A cone is used to signify a wigwam since this activity deals with Native Americans who lived on the plains. The "teams" are now established. Nametags delineate players as "settlers" or as a member of one of the tribes of Native Americans who lived in the plains region.

The rules of the game are now established. When establishing game rules, you need to consider the objectives of the games as well as developmentally appropriate concepts. The purpose of this activity is to allow the students to experience what it was like to be pushed off the land and onto reservations during the westward expansion of America. Analysis of this objective reveals that to do this you need a finite amount of area and two distinct groups. This finite amount of land will be free to both groups at the beginning of the game, but will gradually be taken over by one of the groups forcing the other group on to increasingly smaller parcel of territory. The amount of members on each side will be fixed, eventually leaving one group with more than enough, while the other has to crowd onto the land they are allowed.

After this analysis, I chose a modification of a cooperative games called Musical Hoops (Orlick, 1979). For the purposes of this activity, however, further modifications are required. Musical Hoops is similar to Musical Chairs, except that it removes the concept of elimination. Hoops are spread out on the floor. When music is played the students start moving around among the hoops. When the music stops, the children must find a hoop to enter. Hoops are gradually removed. Instead of having to leave the game, however, if unable to find a hoop, the object of this game if to keep everyone in by sharing the existing hoops. Since the proposed activity requires a finite amount of territory, the number of hoops on the floor must remain constant. In order to achieve the goal then, how the land may be used must be modified. In this case, Native Americans can only use land areas marked by a cone. After each turn, some of the cones are removed, starting in the east and proceeding westward. As land available to the Native Americans becomes scarcer, they are forced to crowd onto the smaller amounts of land remaining, while the settlers have more then enough land available to them. Eventually it will become impossible for the Native American to fit on the land available to them. At this time the groups should switch so each can experience the feelings of injustice and frustration that were felt by the Native Americans during the westward expansion. The teacher can then lead a debriefing of the activity exploring the feelings of the participants.

You can hopefully see and better understand the evolution of an integrated activity using this example. The important point to remember is that you first need to establish your objective. This makes game/activity modification or creation much simpler. A modification checklist and reproducible modification guide are provided on the following pages to assist you in planning and preparing activities.

Activity Modification Checklist

What is the object of the game/activity?

Who/what will the students represent while participating in the activity; e.g., settlers, Native Americans, molecules, animals?

How will the participants be divided; e.g., teams, small groups, partners, individuals. Will this arrangement remain constant or will it change during participation in the activity?

Are there any restrictions concerning how any/all of the players can move?

What type of playing area will be required? Will it have to change in any way during the activity so the objective can be reached?

Is any equipment required? How will it be used to enhance the activity and help the achievement of the activity objective?

How will the activity be debriefed in such a way to assist the students in their understanding of the activity objectives?

References

Helion, J.G. and Fry, F.F. (1995). *Modifying Activities for Developmental Appropriateness.* Journal of Physical Education Recreation and Dance, 66(7), 57-59.

Helion, J.G. and Fry, F.F, (1996) Teaching Cognitive Concepts Through Psychomotor Activities. Kendall Hunt Publishers, Dubuque.

Orlick, T. (1974). The New Games Book. New York: A Dolphin Book/Doubleday.

Soules, M., Barrett, K., Siegal, K. & Little, M. (1994, April). *Developmentally appropriate practices in teaching games.* Presentation at the National Convention of the American Alliance for Health, Physical Education, Recreation and Dance, Denver, CO.

Chapter Seven

The "How to" of Conducting Activities

Chapter Overview

This chapter looks at the teaching methodology and management skills necessary to actually conduct physical activities. Lesson planning, objectives writing, equipment selection, space management are reviewed. Steps for actually implementing such a lesson are also outlined. Reflection and modification options are explored. First aid requirements and safety considerations are also examined.

Questions to Consider

1. What needs to be considered when planning a lesson that uses a physical activity?

2. How does planning differ from what I'm used to?

3. How does available space affect the activity and the equipment used?

4. How do I actually conduct an activity lesson?

5. What should I do in case a child is injured?

Constructing a Game Plan

Any teacher realizes the importance of thorough planning prior to the presentation of a lesson. Physical activities require no less planning. In fact, due to the nature of activities, there will probably be more considerations in the planning. This last statement is not meant to scare off someone who is seriously considering using activities as a means of reinforcing content areas, but is instead meant to make the reader aware that there are additional factors that become important when working in the psychomotor domain.

The Lesson Plan

The actual body of the lesson plan when using physical activities differs little from other lesson planning. Lesson objectives, target audience, choice of equipment, anticipatory set, explanation, guided practice, authentic assessment and closure are very much a part of the activities lesson. The person using an activity needs to be aware of some unique components of this method. (See Appendix 3.)

Objectives

Many classroom teachers, because they work in a classroom, find themselves dealing primarily in the cognitive and affective domains when developing lesson objectives. While activities are used in the classroom, they do not, as a rule, involve large muscle activity or movement over large areas. The use of activities as described in this book, requires that the teacher incorporate a number of new verbs into their repertoire. Whereas cognitive objectives describe what a student will know and affective objectives describe what a student will feel, these new verbs will aid the teacher in describing what the student will be physically able to do. Some examples of these are found on the following page:

build	hit	push	throw
climb	imitate	run	toss
catch	collect	jump	skip
volley	dodge	kick	strike
gallop	leap	swing	shoot
hop	place	tag	

Please be aware that these are only some of the verbs that can be used to create performance objectives in the psychomotor domain, there are others that are also appropriate. As with other types of objectives, psychomotor objects should also include the conditions in which the behavior should be present and the criteria for judging successful performance. (See Appendix 2.)

Factors Affecting Equipment Choices

Once again, equipment concerns are common to all lesson planning. How much is enough? What is appropriate for the activity and the group? How will the equipment be managed? These are some of the questions that typically concern teachers. Type and amount of equipment are determined by considering a number of variables.

Purpose of the Activity

You will want to choose or create equipment that suits the purpose of your activity. There are a number of considerations.

Amount of Space

The size of the space in which an activity will be conducted needs to be considered when planning use of equipment. Available space can be quite variable. Teachers can use classrooms, multi-purpose rooms, gymnasiums, blacktopped playground areas or fields. Each type of area has its own unique characteristics.

Classrooms are the smallest of the areas. Limited space along with pre-existing furniture and/or permanent fixtures makes the use of equipment problematic at times. Equipment needs to be utilitarian and only used if absolutely necessary to the successful conduct of the activity. If used it should be small and unobtrusive so as much existing space as possible can be preserved for safe student movement.

Multi-purpose rooms and gymnasia are much better suited to equipment use. Again, however, because of unique features of some rooms you will encounter, care must be taken when using equipment. Floors of these facilities may be made of vinyl tile, linoleum or wood. Some may even be concrete. In all cases make sure that base type equipment (equipment children will be moving onto and stopping on or moving from) is securely fastened to the floor or is made of a non-skid material. Bases cut from old bath mats work well. Materials can be attached temporarily to the floor with double-sided tape. Whenever using this type of facility make sure that there is adequate space between the walls and any type of equipment.

Blacktopped playground areas do not have the wall problem to consider in some cases, but have other characteristics you need to think about. The rough surface does not allow equipment to be taped in place. Chalk, however, does work quite well for marking of bases and/or boundaries. "Sidewalk Chalk" works the best for this purpose since it is thicker than regular blackboard chalk and comes in a variety of colors that aids visibility. The roughness of blacktopped areas also decreases the useable life of equipment due to high friction and heat.

Fields allow for the use of a great deal of equipment. Because of their nature, however, care must be exercised. Equipment needs to be highly visible. It also needs to be stable due to unevenness of grassy areas. Boundaries are more difficult to define on grass, boundary cones, soda bottle filled with two inches of sand or plastic drinking cups are useful for this purpose. Grass will also remain wet in the mornings, so slipping can be a problem. Field activities are best conducted later in the morning or in the afternoon.

Number of Participants/Groupings

Another factor affecting equipment decisions is the numbers of participants or grouping the planned activity. The larger the size of the group, the more equipment you will require. Depending on the nature of the activity you may need one piece for each participant or one piece for each group. Make sure you know how many groups you will have so sufficient equipment will be available. Manipulation of equipment will have a direct effect on management time.

Types of Movements

Different activities require students to move at different rates of speed and in different directions. Some require that participants "manipulate" the equipment; e.g., throw, catch, kick, roll or hit. Developmentally appropriate equipment should be selected depending on these requirements. As the size of the area opens and increases, the speed at which an activity is conducted can increase. Bases need to be chosen that can be securely placed to prevent slipping and falling. Throwing and catching activities, depending on the age of the participant, can be easy or quite challenging. Equipment that promotes successful completion of the task at hand should be selected. Balloons, scarves, beanbags, yarn balls, foam balls, beachballs, newspaper balls or playground balls can all be used successfully depending on the purpose of the activity, the ability of the participants and the space in which the activity is taking place. Softer equipment should be considered when indoors in a confined space.

Equipment Management

Equipment management can be problematic if the activity you are using requires a good deal of equipment. Often, the specter of moving and setting up a lot of equipment will prevent a person from conducting an activity because of the perceived bother of it all. Also the time required for the set up of a large amount of equipment is also seen as wasted time, since it may take more time to set up an activity then it does to run it.

Large amounts of equipment should not dissuade a person from using an activity. In fact, this is time that can be used to develop cooperation and teamwork among those who will take part in the activity. Delegating the responsibility of equipment distribution, set up and collection to the students gives them a chance to develop a sense of responsibility and a sense of completing a task from beginning to end. It also gives them the opportunity to learn care and proper handling of equipment.

Individual or group tasks must be made quite clear and students should only be assigned to equipment that they can safely handle. Procedures for taking out equipment, distributing or placing equipment as well as collection and storage of equipment must be discussed and responsibilities must be outlined and assigned. This method increases the chances for students to learn responsibility, while reducing management time associated with the activity.

Type and Size of Facility

The type of space you choose for an activity is important if the activity is to have the desired outcomes. Conducting an activity in too small or large a space can prevent students from seeing the bigger purpose of an activity due to such concerns as maneuvering safely in a too small space or dealing with problems of fatigue in a space that is too large. An appropriately chosen area enhances activity, giving students the optimum chance to understand and achieve the planned objectives.

At times there is little or no choice in the setting for an activity. When this is the case certain characteristics of various spaces must be considered. Classrooms are considered small spaces. Classroom furniture, learning stations and other objects commonly found in the classroom combine to take up a large amount of free space. While some if not all of these things are portable, the desirability of moving them may be low. If the classroom is the most commonly used facility, the any activities planned for use there must limit the speed and movement of the participants. Walking activities are most appropriate for a classroom setting. Activities involving tagging, dodging or fast, overt movements can be hazardous for the participants due to the increased risk of collision with furniture objects or other students. Any equipment used in the classroom must be relatively soft so as not to break or damage other classroom furniture or equipment; e.g. foam balls, scarves, balloons (Refer to Previous Section).

Multi-purpose rooms vary in their configuration. Large rooms with high ceilings are quite well suited to a variety of activities. The speed and type of movements that can be used in such rooms are variable since the openness of the room reduces the risk of injury due to collision with furniture, equipment or students. These rooms have other considerations, however. You must still be concerned with any equipment or furniture stored along the walls of these rooms; e.g. lunch tables, milk coolers, pianos, mats, etc. Activity boundaries should also provide a safe distance between the action of the activity and the walls.

Smaller multi-purpose rooms can have other problems in addition to those previously mentioned. Low ceilings, poor lighting, support pillars and heating units are just a few examples. Activities used in these rooms need to be created or modified with the particular configuration of your setting in mind. Both large and small multi-purpose rooms may have tile floors laid over a concrete base. These floors are extremely hard and can cause severe injury if fallen on. Any tag games or other games involving quick changes of direction and sudden stopping need to be carefully planned and supervised to prevent injury to the student.

Outdoor areas, such as playgrounds and fields offer the largest choice of activities. Many of the safety problems associated with indoor spaces are reduced or eliminated. It is important, when using outdoor facilities to use only that portion that lends itself to optimum conduct of the activity. Selecting areas that are too large introduce a fatigue factor that may be detrimental to the overall goal of the activity. If students are overly fatigued they will have a difficult time performing quality movement skills and will also experience difficulty concentrating on the cognitive component of the activity. You may want to plan or modify activities used outdoors to reduce or limit the speed of the activity to address this possible problem. An alternative choice of locomotor skills, such as skipping, galloping or walking can accomplish this task.

Number of Students/Groups

Plan your activities so as many students as possible are actively engaged. Groups should be kept small, having no more than three students. If teams or groupings are used in an activity, each person in the group should be moving most of the time. Relay races or activities that use one or two pieces of equipment for an entire class, such as Spud, Steal the Bacon or Kickball are inappropriate. Structuring groupings so all are involved most of the time increases cognitive engagement and reduces discipline problems. Built-in role changes help to keep interest high while decreasing boredom and fatigue.

Movement Breakdown

How you want the students to move and what you want them to do is important to the success and enjoyment of an activity. While students will want the opportunity to run, your space availability may not allow for this to be done safely. You may also want to limit running and change to another form of locomotion, such as walking, skipping or jogging to make an activity more evenly contested. This will also deal with the problem of fatigue. Throwing and kicking activities have to be carefully planned. Space availability is a key concern as is the ability of the students. Younger children cannot throw or kick as powerfully or as accurately as older children. Activities for younger children should utilize large, colorful targets that they can successfully hit while still being challenged to improve. Activities for older children can use smaller targets. The needs of both groups can be met by using "bull's eye" type targets with feature progressively diminishing concentric circles. If children are throwing objects forcefully or for distance, the object should have some weight to it to prevent injury to the shoulder joint. Beanbags, dense foam balls and yarn balls are better for these types of activities. A policy of "NO HUMAN TARGETS" should be adopted. At no time should children be throwing or kicking any kind of balls or equipment at each other! Dodgeball, Poisonball, Murderball and other such activities are totally inappropriate and are just accidents waiting to happen. There is no way to justify the use of such activities.

Presenting an Activity

Now that you've planned the activity it time to go out and run it with your students. You are used to working in a classroom, but this is a different setting or you are doing something new to you. How does the physical educator do it?

This is a good question and one that prevents many classroom teachers from using activities because they lack a good answer. Teaching an activity is quite similar to teaching in the classroom. There are various steps that are followed in a sequence. First, you need to set up the equipment and the space. Have the students help you do this. Give them specific instructions and use a diagram so they can check that they have set up correctly. Second, call the students together and tell them the name of the activity and the object of the activity. Third, give just enough directions to start the activity. Be specific and give a demonstration of correct and incorrect movements. Fourth, check for understanding by asking questions. Don't get bogged down answering excessive student questions, however. Teach into the activity. Most questions will be answered as the activity progresses. As problems arise during the activity, stop the activity, explain and correct the problem and start playing again. Fifth, modify the activity to make it easier or more challenging as necessary. Give all players the opportunity to experience all roles in the activity. Sixth, stop the activity at a high point. Don't play a game to death.

Students get bored and learn to dislike an activity if this happens. Seventh, have students help you collect and store equipment. This time can be used for to individually think about the activity and what they experienced. Finally, sit the class down after the activity and debrief what happened, how the felt and what they learned.

In Case of Injury

There is always the possibility of injury whenever you have students moving about during an activity. Teachers or other caregivers are responsible to act prudently should an injury occur. A good rule of thumb when dealing with injuries is to be conservative when thinking of the child. In the case of a serious injury or an injury to the head, have the child remain still and send a responsible child to get help. Never leave the class unattended while you go for help. In the case of a non-serious injury, the child may be sent to the office, but should not be sent alone. Another responsible child should accompany the injured child.

In the case of an injury where a child is cut or is bleeding, be sure to follow all of the protocols for dealing with bleeding type injuries. Do not touch the blood or allow any of the other students to come in contact with any blood. Blood protocols should be available through your school district's administration office.

In all cases of injury, follow up by filing an accident report. Be sure the form is filled out promptly; so important details are not forgotten. Explain exactly what happened to the child, but imply no blame or cause.

Reflection

If we are to improve as teachers it is important that we analyze our teaching and choice of activities. It is through this type of reflection that we learn about ourselves and grow in our profession. These are certain questions you may want to consider asking yourself after you have conducted a learning activity.

Was the Activity Fun for All of the Participants?

If the activity was fun and the students enjoyed it, chances are they will like this type of learning activity in the future. If the activity was boring or was just unenjoyable, they will probably balk at this type of methodology.

Did the Activity Accomplish the Intended Goals?

If it did, fine. If not, why didn't it and what can be modified or adapted to assure that activity is successful the next time it is used?

What Changes or Modifications Would Improve This Activity?

Even if an activity went well does not mean that it can't be improved. You should think about the activity and try to identify things that would make it even more fun or more easily understood. You should also ask the participants as part of the debriefing process, exactly what changes they would suggest to make the activity more pleasurable and/or more educational.

What Were the Problems, if Any, Associated with This Activity?

The answer to this question can include things from any area; space, equipment, groupings, rules, movements used in the activity, etc. Observe the activity as it progresses and think carefully about all aspects of it.

How Can These Problems Be Solved?

After identifying the problems associated with an activity, try to rethink ways the activity can be run to alleviate these problems. Changes the boundaries, using different equipment, modifying the rules, creating a larger number of smaller groups or changing the space used are a few ways that activity problems can be solved. Sometimes, a problem arises because students just don't seem to understand what is expected of them. In this case, the teacher needs to look at the explanation of the activity. It needs to be simplified or broken down into smaller, more manageable "chunks" for the students.

The "How to" of conducting activities begins with establishing your objectives in the educational setting. Traditional "busy, happy and good" activities have no place in the effective classroom curriculum. The lesson plan should be the basis for your selection of activities to reinforce the curricular content. The identification of factors surrounding participation by the student should be examined prior to utilization of the activity. Students are our consumers and reflection by the teacher with the help of the students' perceptions can hold the key to successful activity utilization.

Chapter Eight

Obtaining or Making Equipment

Chapter Overview

This chapter explores various ways in which the necessary equipment used to conduct an activity can be obtained. Purchasing, making and borrowing equipment are discussed. Recycling common articles or modifying them to use as activity equipment is also covered. Methods of making common equipment are included. You will find a resource list at the end of the chapter.

Questions to Consider

1. What kinds of equipment needs are anticipated?

2. What resources are at my disposal to obtain this equipment?

3. Can I get help from other teachers, organizations or parents?

What Kinds of Equipment Do I Need?

The activities outlined in this book require a variety of equipment. However, none of the equipment listed is large nor is it necessarily unwieldy. We have tried to include activities that have either modest or manageable equipment requirements. However, there will be some types of equipment that would be beneficial for you to have access.

Balloons	Yarnballs	Clothespins	Foam balls
Jump ropes	Beanbags	Boundary Markers	Targets/Goals
Bases	Balls	Colored Pinnies	Scarves
Beachballs			

This is a suggestion for some basic equipment. Resources, creativity and storage availability will affect the amount of equipment you can accumulate comfortably.

How Can I Get Equipment?

There are four basic methods of obtaining equipment. You can buy equipment, make it, borrow it or recycle other equipment to suit you purposes.

Buying Equipment

Many, if not all, types of equipment mentioned above can be purchased from various sources. Physical Education and Sport equipment catalogues are excellent resources for these purchases. Prices will vary, however, according to the individual vendor, so you should probably check a few sources before making a purchasing decision.

Some of the equipment is available at some of your local stores. Home centers, supermarkets and discount stores will often have various pieces of equipment available for purchase. Clothespins and clotheslines are two examples. The resources tend to be less expensive than equipment companies and are generally more convenient. You need to check the quality of the equipment you are purchasing, however.

It is more convenient and less expensive to buy some items in bulk. Balloons are much less expensive if bought by the gross. Buying one long rope and cutting it into a number of short ropes will also save you money. Material stores sell yards of scarf material that can be cut into a number of scarves as opposed to buying them individually.

Combining resources is always a good idea. If a number of teachers in a particular school are interested in developing and using psychomotor activities, all can contribute to the purchase of the equipment and it can be shared. This option increases purchase power, while decreasing the amount of space necessary for storage. Activities need to be coordinated among the different users, however, to ensure that equipment will be available when needed.

Making Equipment

Some of the equipment can be easily made. Scarves and jump ropes were earlier mentioned as two such examples, however, beanbags, yarnballs, other kinds of balls, boundary markers and targets are others. These are methods of making other kinds of equipment.

Beanbags
Materials: heavy clothe, plastic beads, sewing machine
1. Cut 5" x 10" rectangles from a large piece of heavy material.
2. Fold the rectangle in half to form a 5" square.
3. Sew up two side of the square, leaving one side open.
4. Turn the bag inside out and fill half full with **plastic beads**.
   (Real beans attract mice!)
5. Tuck in and sew closed the remaining side.

Yarnballs
Materials: Yarn, cardboard, string or wire
1. Make two cardboard circles approximately 4" in diameter. Cut a 1" hole in the center of the circles.
2. Place the circles on top of each other and wrap them with yarn until the are almost filled.
3. Cut the yarn along the outermost edge of the circle.
4. Slightly separate the two cardboard circles and secure the yarn in the center using string or wire. *Make sure the yarn is fastened tightly!*

5. Remove the cardboard circles and comb or fluff out the yarn ball.

Foam Balls
Materials: 6" to 12" cubes of foam (These can be cut from a large 6" to 12" piece of foam, which is available at many material or craft stores)
1. Use a sharp knife to cut off the eight corners off the cube.

Newspaper Balls/Trashballs
Materials: Newspaper, masking tape
1. Ball up two or three sheets of newspaper. For trashballs, ball up an over sized plastic garbage bag. (Lawn bags work well for this purpose.)
2. Wrap the newspaper ball or trashbag with masking tape until completely covered.

Boundary Markers/Targets
Materials: 1 and 2 liter plastic soda bottles, gallon milk jugs, sand, electrician's tape
1. Fill bottles with 2 inches of sand.
2. Tightly recap the bottles.
3. Securely tape caps in place.

Jump Ropes
Material: 100 ft. of heavy clothesline, electrician's tape
1. Launder clothesline 2 or three times to remove stiffness.
2. Cut rope into 7' and 8' lengths.
3. Tape ends of rope to prevent fraying.

These are just a few examples of how to make equipment. Many more types of equipment can be made quite easily. There are a number of resources available.

Borrowing Equipment

In many cases, much of the equipment needed for many activities is already in the school. Many times the school's physical educator has already purchased the equipment and is knowledgeable regarding various ways in which it can be used. If this is the case, the individual teacher or group of teachers can approach the physical education specialist to set up a system in which equipment can be borrowed and used by the classroom teachers.

Guidelines for Borrowing Equipment
1. Make sure you secure permission from the Physical Educator and Principal before borrowing any equipment.
2. Request for permission to borrow equipment well in advance, to make sure it is not being used by the physical educator or another teacher.
3. Treat the equipment with respect. Handle it properly (if unsure how equipment should be used, ask.). Replace anything damaged or broken.
4. Note how and where the equipment is stored when you pick it up. Replace it in the same manner when you return it.

Some teachers will be more willing than others to share equipment. These decisions are not usually personal. Many factors go into the decision as to whether or not a person is able to share equipment. Make sure you understand these reasons in order to prevent any adverse feelings or morale problems in your setting.

Recycling Other Materials

Various items not originally intended for use in physical activities actually work wonderfully when used in that way. I have already mentioned how soda bottles and milk jugs can be used, but there are others.

Carpet Squares
These are usually available at carpet retailers. Books of carpet samples are usually just discarded. Contact the various retailers in your area and ask if they will let you have them. They can be used as bases and seat mats.

Bowling Pins
Bowling alleys are usually willing to give their discarded bowling pins away. These make good boundary markers and targets. They tend to be noisy, however, so they should be used where they will not disturb anyone else.

Broomsticks/Mop Handles

These can be cut down to make various sized sticks and wands.

#10 Cans

These are the large aluminum or tin cans used in cafeterias. Ask the people in your cafeteria to save these for you. They make good targets and are useful for storing small items.

Again, these are just some examples. What can be recycled is only limited to your needs and your imagination. Try to look for the potential use of various items. Make sure, however, they are appropriate for the use intended and are safe.

References

Corbin, Charles B. and Corbin, David E.[1981] Homemade Play Equipment. American Press, Boston, MA

Equipment resources/suppliers:

Cramer Products, Inc.
150 N. McQuesten Parkway
Mt. Vernon, NY 10550

Gopher Sports
2929 West Park Drive
Owatonna, MN

Palos Sports
12235 S. Harlem Ave.
Palos Heights, IL 60463

Snitz, Mfg. Co.
P.O. Box 76
East Troy, WI 53120

Things From Bell
P.O. Box 206
Princeton, WI 54968

U.S. Games
1901 Diplomat Drive
Dallas, TX 75234

Flaghouse, Inc.,
153 W. Warren, P.O. Box 1001
Gardner, KS 66030

Mohinder Sports
2574 Industrial Rowe
Turlock, CA 95380

Passon's Sports
P.O.Box 49
Jenkintown, PA 19046

/Chime Time/ Jugglebug
One Sporttime Way
Atlanta, GA 30340-1402

Toledo Physical Education Supply
P.O. Box 5618
Toledo, OH 43613

Appendices

Appendix 1
Cooperative Map Drawing Activity

This activity can be conducted either indoors or outdoors depending on your particular situation.

Outdoor Procedures

Equipment: String, Chalk (Sidewalk chalk works best), Tape measure, rulers or yardsticks, Map grid for all students.

Procedures: This can be a teacher directed project or can be conducted as a problem solving activity. Your choice depends on the ability of the group you are working with.
1.   Tell the students that they will be transferring the drawing the map onto the playground.
2.   Have the students draw the grid on the ground using a designated measurement for the squares, e.g. 1, 2 or 3 feet. Students should calculate the required length of each grid line. These lengths should be measured off and drawn. Stretching a length of string between points and drawing along the string keeps the lines straight.
3.   Have students transfer the each section of the map from the paper grid onto the corresponding larger grid on the ground. (Reference marks on the grid lines and in the grids where state lines cross it helps in this process.)
4.   Have the students identify each state.
5.   Debrief the activity by exploring what processes the students used to work together to solve the problem of the map transfer. Ask about decision-making procedures, task assignment, leadership roles, feeling of success/frustration and teamwork and cooperation.

Indoor Procedures

Rather than drawing a grid, give each student or group of students a large piece of poster board or other heavy drawing paper. Each section of the grid is transferred to a piece of the paper. When finished the students can put the pieces together like a jigsaw puzzle. A key factor in the success of this project is for students working on adjoining grid sections getting together to create common crossover points for their grids

A related activity after the map is drawn would be to break the class into small groups and have them create an activity that uses the map. You can ask the children to incorporate different subject areas; i.e., geography, mathematics, etc.

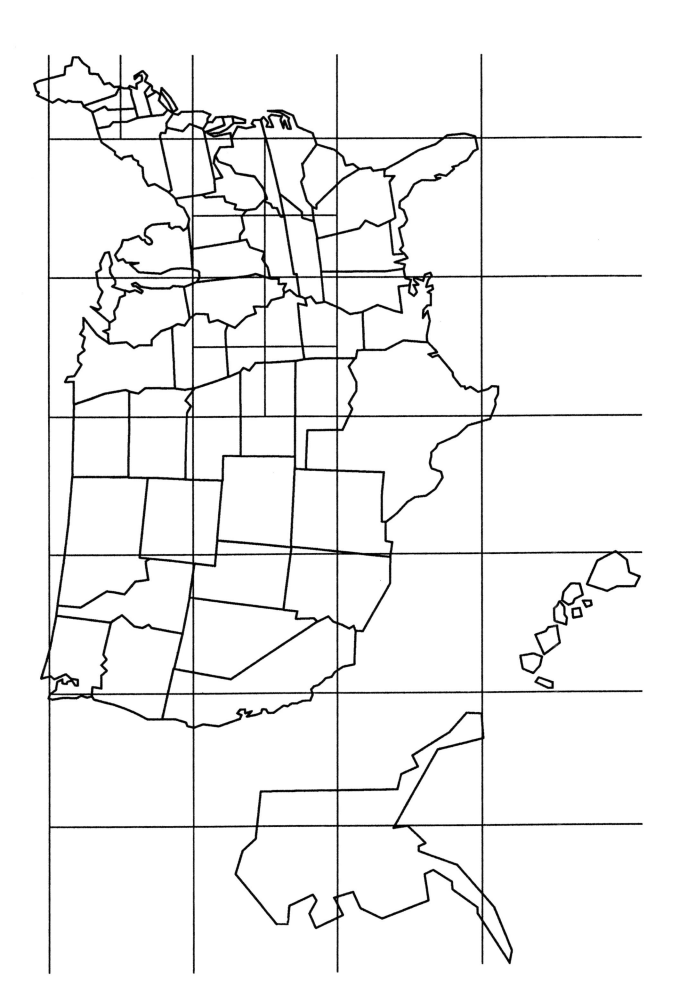

Appendix 2
Performance Objective Worksheet

Performance Objectives Worksheet

Planning for student outcomes involves planning on the part of the teacher. The teacher must map out a direction for the individual lesson, the unit and the curriculum. To begin the teacher must ask three significant questions: Where am I going? How will I get there? and How will I know when I have arrived?

Performance objectives should be written in terms of the student learning outcomes anticipated as a result of participation in the lessons' activities.

"An instructional objective is a statement describing a task, the conditions under which it will be performed, and the criteria or standards by which it will be judged to have been completed successfully. Instructional objectives are often referred to as behavioral or performance objectives" (Siedentop, 1991:199).

The requirements for writing a performance objective include:
the **behavior** component to an instructional objective is written as a verb that describes what the student is to do;
the **condition** component of an instructional objective describes the situation under which the action will be performed;
the **criterion** component of an objective describes minimal levels of performance for the action specified (Rink, 1993).

> *Criteria are usually specified in two ways: (1) as quantitative criteria, which usually deal with the effectiveness of the movement response or other behavior, such as how many, how long, how high, how far; or (2) as qualitative criteria, which deal with the process characteristics of the movement, such as the form of the movement. Process characteristics describe the extent to which the student is doing the movement correctly, such as stepping into the swing, getting into position, or showing the characteristics of mature form (Rink, 1996:208).*

"There are two ways of making instructional [performance] objectives for any given task more or less difficult: (1) by manipulating the conditions under which the task is performed and (2) by manipulating the criteria by which the task will be judged" (Siedentop, 1991:201).

Objectives are generally written in the psychomotor domain to reflect product criteria, however is perfectly acceptable to utilize some form of process criteria when appropriate.

References

Harrison, J.M., Blackmore, C.L., Buck, M.M. & Pellett, T.L. (1996). *Instructional Strategies for Secondary School Physical Education (*4th Ed.). Chicago: Brown & Benchmark Publishers.

Rink, Judith E. (1993). *Teaching Physical Education for Learning* (2nd Ed.). St. Louis: Mosby.

Siedentop, Daryl (1991). *Developing Teaching Skills in Physical Education* (3rd Ed.). Mountain View, CA: Mayfield Publishing Company.

Randall, Lynda E. (1992). *Systematic Supervision for Physical Education.* Champaign, Illinois: Human Kinetics Publishers.

Wuest, D. & Bennett Lomabard (1994). *Curriculum and Instruction: The Secondary School Physical Education Experience.* St. Louis: Mosby.

Performance Objectives Worksheet

#1 Follow the suggested format:

Identify the *Behavior*:

_____

The **behavior** portion of the performance objective should include some type of concrete action, which describes what the student, will be "doing" during the lesson activity. Words such as: reciting, listing, performing, throwing, skipping, etc. provide some activity by which the teacher can visualize participation. The use of vague terminology such as, knowing, learning, appreciating, etc. should be avoided since the teacher cannot determine when the students fulfill these requirements.

Select the *Condition*_____

The **condition** portion should outline the parameter surround participation in the lesson's activity. Conditions could be: with a partner, in a small group, as a member of a team, written on piece of paper, standing on a base, before returning to active participation, etc. These conditions should assist the teacher in defining how the student will meet the performance objective.

Set the *Criteria*_____

The **criteria** may be quantitative (3 out of 4, within 15 seconds, etc.) or qualitative (continuously, without missing, using correct form, etc.). The criteria should set the standard or determine how well the student must perform so the teacher can determine the success or failure of the lesson's learning outcomes.

Write the *performance objective* in statement form:

_____
_____
_____

#2
Identify the *Behavior*_____

Select the *Condition*_____

Set the *Criteria*_____

Write the performance objective in statement form:

_____
_____
_____

Appendix 3
Activity Planning Worksheets

Name of Game

Focus:

Summary:

Success criteria:

Activity diagram: If

Activity description:

Equipment requirements:

Teacher's notes:

Name of Game

Focus:

Summary:

Success criteria:

Activity diagram: If

Activity description:

Equipment requirements:

Teacher's notes:

Index

Dr. Helion is an associate professor in the Department of Kinesiology at West Chester University of Pennsylvania. He earned his Bachelors degree form the State University of New York at Cortand in the field of Physical Education. He earned his Masters and Doctoral degrees from Teachers College, Columbia University in the area of Curriculum and Teaching in Movement Sciences. He has taught physical education at elementary, secondary and university levels. He has published articles in national journals and has presented at the international and national levels. His primary responsibilities and interests include teacher preparation, curriculum development, assessment and experiential education. He is especially concerned with the development of an emotionally and physically safe learning environment for students. He lives ion West Chester, PA with his wife Ann, an elementary level principal and his daughters Courtney and Chelsea.

Dr. Fry is currently an associate professor in the Department of Kinesiology at West Chester University of Pennsylvania. He received his undergraduate education in Health and Physical Education at West Chester. He completed his Masters degree at the University of Colorado at Greeley and completed his doctorate at Springfield College. He works in the teacher education program, preparing students in the fields of Health and Physical Education. He has worked at the elementary, secondary and university levels, including Thomond College of Education in Ireland. He has presented workshops and in-service programs at regional and national levels on the modification of activities to enhance developmental appropriateness and reinforcement of cognitive content. He is currently working on creating developmentally appropriate activities in experiential education. He lives in Wilmington, Delaware with his wife, Marcia, an elementary educator and his sons Tyler and Kyle.